STORIES FROM
The Swedish Heritage

Arland O. Fiske

i

International Standard Book Number: 0-942323-17-3

Cover design by
Sheldon Larson of Creative Media, Minot, ND.

Cover photo by
Jim Turner, Turner Photography, Lindsborg, Kansas.

The children on the cover are
Miles and Emily Ekenberry
of Lindsborg, Kansas.

Published by
North American Heritage Press
A DIVISION OF
CREATIVE MEDIA, INC.
P.O. Box 1
Minot, North Dakota 58702
701/852-5552

Printed in the United States of America

Dedication

*To my many
Swedish friends
and especially
to those
who have
perpetuated
their heritage
in America.*

STORIES FROM THE SWEDISH HERITAGE

CONTENTS

PART II
SWEDEN AND THE SWEDISH HERITAGE
IN THE 'NEW WORLD'

PART II
THE HERITAGE SHARED WITH THEIR
SCANDINAVIAN NEIGHBORS

STORIES FROM THE SWEDISH HERITAGE

FOREWORD

IN THIS COLLECTION OF STORIES, Arland O. Fiske brings to the reader a rich variety of subjects on Sweden and Swedish-America. Since the great Swedish migration to America between 1840 and 1914, our two countries have been linked in many ways. The author explores this heritage through accounts of Sweden, of its people and history, and of the immigrants and their contributions to America.

The author presents us with a veritable cornucopia. Here we read of Fredrika Bremer's 1849 visit to America, of Swedish settlements in Kansas, Texas, and New York, of the Wasa ship museum in Stockholm, of Nobel Prize winning author Selma Lagerlöf – and even of the exploding interest of golf in Sweden! These are stories of a shared history and of exemplary individuals (some well-known, others less so) which have importance to us all.

Arland Fiske brings an informed and curious mind to these varied topics. He writes engagingly about Sweden and Swedish-America, past and present, revealing his affection and love for the Scandinavian peoples. This is a book that one will want to return to time and again.

– Bruce N. Karstadt
  Executive Director
  The American Swedish Institute
  Minneapolis, Minnesota

STORIES FROM THE SWEDISH HERITAGE

PREFACE

THIS BOOK CONTAINS TWO KINDS OF STORIES, all of them related to Sweden and the Swedish people. Some of the stories are specifically Swedish and others portray the place of Sweden and Swedish people in the larger world of their sphere of influence. These relate to their Scandinavian neighbors to the west and to Finland in the east, plus the Baltics and even into Russia.

These stories originally appeared in a syndicated column and were intended as vignettes to interest the reader in the Scandinavian lore. The stories in this book have been previously published with the exception of two: The one on Gov. Hugo Anderson and the other on Scandinavian Humor. The previously published stories were included in *The Scandinavian Heritage* (1987), *The Scandinavian World* (1988), *The Scandinavian Spirit* (1989), and *The Scandinavian Adventure* (1990).

There have been inquiries for a book on just Swedish and Swedish related stories. A similar book published as *The Best of the Norwegian Heritage* (1990) has been well received. It has been the encouragement of my Swedish friends that has led me to publish this volume. There are more stories which ought to be included under the title, *Stories From The Swedish Heritage* and I hope to write many of them as time for research allows. These have been written because of the appeal they have made to me.

Sweden and the Swedish people around the world have made contributions far beyond what one would expect of a nation of only 8,500,000 people. Unlike the days of emigration when Sweden was largely rural, today eighty-four percent live in urban areas. A population of only a little over 9,000,000 is projected by the year 2010. The average life expectancy is seventy-four years for males and eighty years for females. This denotes a very high standard of living and health care.

Sweden's economy is bolstered by high taxes and many social benefits. Forty percent of Sweden's national budget is spent on health, social affairs and education. Less than ten percent is spent on defense. While tourists spend almost $2,500,000,000 per year in Sweden, Swedes spend over $4,500,000,000 abroad. This reflects the strength of the Swedish krone (crown). Sweden's national debt is about 80 billion in U.S. dollars.

Sweden has a vigorous and diversified economy. Imports include machinery and transport equipment, chemicals, food and tobacco products, clothing and footwear. Exports include machinery and transport equipment (e.g. Saab and Volvo autos), paper products, wood and wood pulp, chemicals, and iron and steel products. Their major trade partner is Germany, following by the United States, Great Britain, Norway, Finland and Denmark. Their balance of trade shows that they are a creditor nation.

The Swedish people are well informed on world affairs. One hundred seventy-five newspapers have a daily circulation of almost five million. There is almost one radio per person, two television sets per five persons, and one telephone per person.

For further information the reader is directed to Lilly Lorenzen's *Of Swedish Ways* and to *Sweden: The Nation's History* by Franklin D. Scott. There are other helpful references too, including the articles in the encyclopedia Britannica.

I'm indebted to many people for making this book possible: First of all to my wife, Gerda, who has been my chief inspiration, together with our children and grandchildren; to Bruce Karstadt, Executive Director of the American Swedish Institute, for writing the Foreword; to Dr. Edward Lindell, former president of Gustavus Adolphus College, for his critical reading of the manuscript and suggestions. Special thanks are due to Allen O. Larson and the North American Heritage Press for making this book possible; to Tammy Wolf for preparing the text for publication; to Sheldon Larson for designing the cover; and to my daughter, Lisa Gaylor, for drawing the illustrations. Thanks to Miles and Emily Ekenberry of Lindsboro, Kansas, for gracing the cover and to all the readers who keep the heritage alive in the New World.

–Arland O. Fiske, Kabekona Lake, Laporte, Minnesota
    September 18, 1991 - Remembrance Day for
    Dag Hammarskjold (1905-1961), Peacemaker

PART I

*Sweden
And The
Swedish Heritage
In The
'Old World'*

CHAPTER 1

The
Swedish Spirit

S WEDEN IS THE LARGEST of the Scandinavian countries, with 173,630 square miles (a little larger than California) and has over eight million people. It stretches for one thousand miles north to south and is 350 miles wide in parts. Sweden is well represented in the New World too. During the immigration period, from about 1840 to 1920, twenty-five percent of its population left the old country.

The visitor to Sweden is impressed with the beautiful countryside, its productive farms and clean woodlands. Ninety-six thousand lakes plus rivers and canals are a part of its land surface. Stockholm, the capital city, is a wonderland for people who like castles and palaces. The country's wealth is clearly visible. Sweden has one of the highest economic standards of living in the world.

Why is this possible? Sweden has not been in a war since 1814 and that was only a border skirmish with Norway. Unlike Denmark and Norway which were involved in World War II against their wishes, Sweden managed to maintain neutrality. It was not without a price. The Nazis everywhere violated this neutrality. Yet, the Swedes gave much needed support to the resistance movements in both of those occupied countries. Swedish leaders, like Count Folke Bernadotte, negotiated the release of many from Nazi prison camps. Sweden also became a haven for Danish Jews in October 1943.

In the old Viking days, Swedes made their mark on Russia and were famous in Constantinople as the Emperor's body guard. In later days, Swedish kings pushed their way on to the continent of Europe and occupied parts of the Baltic region and northern Germany. But since 1809, Sweden has been a constitutional monarchy. Today, the king is a symbol of the Swedish spirit more than a ruler. He has no power except the persuasion of his example and personal charisma. But it seems to work well and the royal family is very popular among the people. Likewise, the once powerful nobility no longer have special privileges. They do possess much of the country's wealth, but are respected more than envied.

Sweden and the Swedish people around the world have made contributions far beyond what one would expect of a nation of only 8,500,000 people. Unlike the days of emigration when Sweden was largely rural, today eighty-four percent live in urban areas. A population of only a little over nine million is projected by the year 2010. The average life expectancy is seventy-four years for males and eighty years for females.

Sweden's economy is bolstered by high taxes and many social benefits. Forty percent of Sweden's national budget is spent on health care, social programs and education. Less than ten percent is spent on defense. While tourists spend two and a half billion per year in Sweden, Swedes spend over four and a half billion abroad. This reflects the strength of the Swedish krona (crown). Sweden's national debt is about eight billion in U.S. dollars. There has, however, been some resistance to its generous welfare policies by the voters. It remains to be seen what the outcome will be.

Sweden has a vigorous and diversified economy. Imports include machinery and transport equipment, chemicals, food and tobacco products, clothing and footwear. Exports include machinery and transport equipment also (e.g. Saab and Volvo autos, buses and trucks), wood and wood products, chemicals, and iron and steel products. Their major trade partners include Germany, the United States, Great Britain, Norway, Finland and Denmark, in that order. In the balance of trade they are a creditor nation.

The Swedish people are well informed on world affairs. One hundred seventy-five newspapers have a daily circulation of almost five million. There is one radio and one telephone per person, and two television sets per five persons.

The visitor to Sweden cannot help but notice that there are no slums. On a tour of the old part of Stockholm, I saw an old man rummaging through a trash can. The guide told us that he was a "deviate," probably a "wino." She said: "No one in Sweden has to do that." The Swedes, however, very jealously guard their country against "freeloaders." A few years ago, our daughter, Lisa, was travelling through Sweden to Norway, but did not have her return plane ticket to America (we had it and were planning to meet her in Oslo). The customs officers questioned her for an hour before she convinced them that she was not planning to illegally remain in Sweden and take advantage of their welfare system designed to help the poor.

The Swedes are a friendly people with hospitable manners, clean homes and a feeling for what is right and beautiful. Freedom brings problems too, but they try to keep these matters within the law. Quality workmanship is found in their manufactured products. If you have never been to Sweden, the next best thing to do is to become friends with some Swedish-Americans who have kept their traditions alive in the New World.

SWEDEN AND THE SWEDISH HERITAGE IN THE 'OLD WORLD'

CHAPTER 2

Sweden – Its
People And Royalty

FIFTEEN THOUSAND YEARS AGO, Sweden, like most of northern Europe, was covered by a glacier. That's not a long time in geological history. About nine thousand years ago, fishermen and hunters began to settle in Sweden. Then about 2,500 years ago, another Ice Age began which lasted four hundred years. The present inhabitants of Sweden, as well as Denmark and Norway, are a part of the Teutonic migration that came from Germany.

The center of power in early Sweden was the "Svea" tribe near Uppsala. The name "Sweden" is derived from them. Many historians also identify the "Goths" who spread over Europe to have originally migrated from Sweden. There's one thing about people that is for certain – they are always on the move.

Once the center of Viking activity, Swedish traders and soldiers of fortune travelled eastward into Russia and then southward to Constantinople. They established the first kingdom of Russia at Kiev and many became known as "Varangians," the Greek emperor's elite palace guard. The word, "Varangian," is of Scandinavian origin and refers to "confederates" or who have pledged themselves to another. The name "Rus," modern "Russia," originally referred to Sweden.

In the Viking days, the worship of Odin, Thor and Frey, struck terror in the hearts of the people because of their great appetite for human sacrifice. It was the Christian missionaries from Germany and England who gave them new directions.

In 1397, Sweden was joined to Denmark and Norway in the Union of Kalmar. In 1523, the Vasa family came to power and created an independent Sweden. They also established the Lutheran Reformation. The most famous of the Vasa kings was Gustav II Adolf, more commonly referred to as Gustavus Adolphus. Swedish immigrants founded a college at St. Peter, Minnesota, after his name in 1862.

7

SWEDEN AND THE SWEDISH HERITAGE IN THE 'OLD WORLD'

The Vasa family ran out of heirs in the early 1800s and made an agreement with Napoleon to invite his Marshall, Jean Baptiste Jules Bernadotte, to become the crown prince. He accepted and took the name "Karl Johan." Then he switched sides over to the British for which he was rewarded by being given Norway by the Treaty of Kiel (1814). He was not Norway's choice of king, but did prove to be a good ruler for them.

The Bernadottes continue as the royal family of Sweden and are very popular both in Sweden and among Swedes in America. The present king, Carl XVI Gustaf, was given solid academic preparation for his ceremonial position. His wife, Sylvia, is of German and Brazilian background. King Harald V of Norway is also a Bernadotte through his mother, the late Crown Princess Martha.

Sweden has had peace since 1814 and this contributes towards its great progress in science, statesmanship, and for its leadership in Christian humanitarianism. This is also why so much of Sweden's magnificent architecture of the past remains for us to see when we visit Stockholm. In 1976, Sweden elected a non-socialist Prime Minister and continues its cautious neutralist policies. In a world of so much conflict, there is much we can learn from the Swedes.

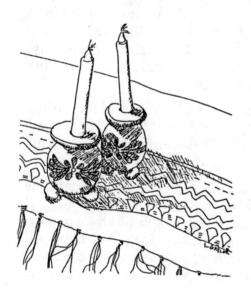

Swedish candlesticks.

CHAPTER 3

Stockholm's
'Gamla Stan'

ONE OF THE QUAINTEST PLACES to visit in Scandinavia is "Gamla Stan" (Old Town) in Stockholm, Sweden. It's built up around the royal palace. A fortification was erected there about 1150 for the city's defense. The present palace was completed in 1760. It's now a museum open to visitors. The royal family has chosen to live where they have more privacy.

Sixty-eight places of interest are pointed out to visitors on this peninsula connected with bridges leading to the city's main shopping area to the north. It contains some of the most interesting old buildings in Sweden. Many have been restored and are used for businesses. We stayed in the Reisen Hotel along the east edge of Gamla Stan which overlooks the waterway that connects with the Baltic Sea. Through the hotel window, we saw ocean liners coming in to dock and ferries transporting people to their homes on the many islands which make up the metropolitan area of Sweden's capital city. On a nice day, sailboats are cutting the waves.

We went on a walking tour through Gamla Stan. Next to the palace was the Storkyrkan (Cathedral) with its famous statue of St. George and the Dragon, a favorite mythology of Scandinavia. As we passed the German Church, we visited with a man coming out from the fenced enclosure. He told us that Stockholm has had a large German community since about 1600. German is the second language for many of the city's inhabitants. It's no secret that during World War I the Swedish king favored his German wife's homeland. In World War II, the royal family, however, detested Hitler and gave whatever help they could to both Denmark and Norway. There is also a Finnish Church just south of the Cathedral. Finland was ruled by Sweden for about six hundred years. Travel between the lands is still popular, especially on the Silja Line, an overnight trip by sea.

SWEDEN AND THE SWEDISH HERITAGE IN THE 'OLD WORLD'

A few blocks to the west is Riddar Holmen, an island that is now connected to Gamla Stan. In the thirteenth century, it was the home of Franciscan monks who built a cloister. One of the famous names in Stockholm and on this island is Birger Jarl who founded the city. His statue was erected in 1854 and occupies a commanding position.

It's a good idea to have your camera handy when you visit these historic sites. Not only are there many unusual examples of architecture, but you can get a good history lesson just from seeing the statues which seem to be everywhere. This is particularly true in Stockholm, because there hasn't been a military battle in the city for over 460 years.

Gamla Stan has a variety of small shops which are international in character. The Swedish crown had been devalued when we were there in 1985 so that American money went a long way. We also got our money's worth because Swedish craftmanship is famous for its quality, especially crystal, furs, woolen clothing and steel products. I usually look for book stores and I was not disappointed. The krona has rebounded and made good purchasing value by 1992.

It's a wonder that this area has been so well preserved. Fires have destroyed many of the original buildings. But the Swedes are proud of their past and have spent the necessary money to rebuild historical sites. If you want to see the best of an old Swedish city, a visit to Gamla Stan alone is worth the trip to this great and beautiful country.

CHAPTER 4

Stockholm's
'Storkyrkan'

"STOR-KYRKAN" MEANS "THE BIG CHURCH." That's what people in Stockholm, Sweden, call St. Nicholas' Cathedral. Begun about 1250, it was the only church in the city for almost four hundred years, except for monastery chapels.

Stockholm is a city of foureen islands, forty bridges and many beautiful canals. The cathedral is located next to the royal palace in "Gamla Stan" ("Old Town"). The streets are so narrow at places that you can touch the buildings on both sides as you walk through. Visiting this island is a must for every tourist to Sweden's capital city. Selma Lagerlof, the famed Swedish novelist, called Stockholm "the city that floats on water."

Surrounded by the palace and other royal buildings, Storkyrkan has witnessed many of Sweden's most important events, including the coronations of its kings and queens, royal weddings and funerals. Coronations, however, are no longer held in Sweden, as they are considered too expensive.

Come inside this great church with me for a closer look. It has five aisles. About half way up the middle aisle is the high pulpit. It's almost three hundred years old and is heavily adorned with works of art. I was impressed with the heavy overlay of gold and the hour glass which the preacher flips over when he begins the sermon. He stops preaching when all the sand has run through.

Right across the aisle from the pulpit is the burial place of Olaus Petri (d. 1552), who brought the Lutheran Reformation to Sweden. There is also a memorial to Archbishop Nathan Soderblom, one of Sweden's best known churchmen.

The most interesting statue in the cathedral is of St. George, a very popular saint of the Middle Ages. The legends tell us that he was a knight in Cappadocia (Asia Minor). One day he came to a town in Libya (North Africa) where a dragon was terrorizing the people. Each day they had to feed it two sheep. When they ran out of sheep, the dragon demanded humans to eat. Victims were chosen by lots. St. George arrived on the day the lot fell on the king's only daughter. Hearing of her danger, he rode to her rescue.

Capturing the beast, he led it back into the city. When the royal family and the people agreed to become Christians, he killed the dragon. Knight George was martyred by the Emperor Diocletion (about A.D. 303) After his death, many miracles were claimed to have been worked in his name. The statue of St. George, protector of Sweden, was erected to celebrate a Swedish victory over the Danes in 1471. Our guide told us that the Princess' statue represented Sweden and the dragon was Denmark. At that time, Denmark ruled over both Norway and Sweden.

There are many more interesting things to see in Storkyrkan, including a huge painting of the Crucifixion above the altar and a beautifully carved crucifix. What especially interested me, however, was a large wrought-iron globe representing Swedish foreign missions. When people make donations to missions, they light a candle to represent their gift. It was well lit. The next time I visit the cathedral, I'm going to light a candle too.

CHAPTER 5

Sten Sture –
A Swedish Hero

FIVE HUNDRED YEARS AGO, there lived in Sweden a family named "Sture." They were among the most powerful people of the land from 1470-1520. In fact there were three Stures who governed. Two of them were named "Sten," Sten the Elder and Sten the Younger. Between them, Svante Nilsson Sture ruled. Sten the Younger was Svante's son.

It's easy to idealize the past and think, "How nice it would have been to have lived in the good old days." Reading even a little bit of history can be a good cure for this kind of mistaken nostalgia. When I read about the "good old days," I'm thankful to be living today, even with the serious threats of a nuclear holocaust, AIDS and other horrifying dangers to life. How could it have been so dangerous for people in the "isolated" northlands of Scandinavia?

In 1380, Margaret I, a Danish Princess who had become the Queen of Norway, began a rule that gathered Norway, Denmark and Sweden into one kingdom through the Treaty of Kalmar (Sweden) signed on July 13, 1397. Margaret lived for another fifteen years and was the virtual ruler even though she was not the official sovereign.

The Norwegians and Danes remained one until 1814, but the Swedes had long before broken with the Treaty of Kalmar. One of the colorful rulers of Sweden was Karl Knutsson (intermittently king from 1448 to 1470) who was elected monarch three times, probably a world record. He was caught in a power play between the Kalmar Treaty and the Danish king, the German merchants known as the Hanseatic League, the church representing the influence of Rome, and the Swedish Council which had the power to elect and dispose. The Council members, comprised of the wealthy nobility, were always looking out for themselves. It was a cloak and dagger political situation in which nobody trusted anyone else.

SWEDEN AND THE SWEDISH HERITAGE IN THE 'OLD WORLD'

Sten Sture the Elder (1440-1503), a nephew of King Karl, was a trusted lieutenant of the king. When the king died in 1470, Sten made his move for power. He threw a big party on Walpurgis Eve 1471 (April 30) for the townsmen and peasants. He served 5,000 pints of strong German beer, after which they acclaimed him "regent" (governor). His rival was Denmark's King Christian I, who claimed the right to rule Sweden because of the Kalmar Treaty signed 73 years earlier. The showdown took place on a hill called "Brunkeberg" on October 10, 1471, in what is now downtown Stockholm. The hill has been since leveled for homes and skyscrapers.

Sten Sture won a bloody battle and hired a famous German sculptor named Bernt Notke to make a statue of St. George slaying a dragon which was about to devour the king's daughter (Stockholm). Sten himself posed for the statue of St. George. The dragon represented Denmark and King Christian. The imposing wooden statue now may be seen in the Stockholm Cathedral (Storkyrkan). I admit to having been impressed with both the statue and the story. One of Sten's significant achievements was the founding of the University of Uppsala in 1477, a prestigious center of learning.

The balance of power shifted between the Danish kings and the Swedish dissenters to the Kalmar Treaty. Even without royal lineage or title, Sten Sture was the chief power in Sweden for almost 30 years. Nobody claims that he was virtuous. He had no respect for morality or truth. He both supported and plundered churches and was twice excommunicated by the Pope. Still Sweden prospered under him and he was probably no more Machiavellian than other rulers of his time. Vilhelm Moberg (best known for his book *Emigrants*) called Sten the Elder a master of "realpolitik" (the politics of reality) in his book *A History of the Swedish People*. Fate finally caught up with Sten. In good health, he suddenly died, probably from poison slipped into his drink by his successor's fiancee.

His successor, Svante Nilsson (1440-1512), ruled for eight less eventful years. Svante's son, Sten Sture the Younger (1492-1520), was one of Sweden's more interesting rulers. Named a knight at age four, Sten the Younger knew how to appeal to the common

14

people for support. Ruthless like other rulers of his time, he was nonetheless a man of action and knew where he was going. Apart from the Danish kings, his chief opposition came from Bishop Trolle. It was not uncommon in those days for bishops to lead armies and claim political as well as spiritual power.

The conflict between the regent and the bishop led to the invasion of Sweden by an army of German mercenaries in the service of the Danish King to punish Sten. Sten was cut down at age twenty-seven by a Danish musket ball and died on February 3, 1520. His conflict with the bishop was finally resolved in the infamous Stockholm "Bloodbath" of November 8, 1520. Having been declared a "heretic," his body was exhumed and publicly burned while eighty-two men were beheaded in the public square by the castle. The bloodbath travelled to Finland, then ruled by Sweden, where more people, including monks and children, were executed.

The Danish king's position looked safe, but the bloodbath only stirred the Swedish determination to throw out the Danes which they did under the leadership of Gustav Vasa who carried out the Sture policies. After the final breakup of their Union, Sweden and Denmark fought eleven wars between 1563 and 1814. The Sture family is now extinct, but one of its branches, the Oxenstiernas, has continued to be one of Sweden's most famous aristocratic dynasties. Today, both Denmark and Sweden are among the world's greatest promoters of peace.

Those are interesting days to read about, but I would not liked to have lived in them. Maybe it's better not to know too much about our ancient ancestors. You can never tell how many skeletons and ghosts are hidden in the closets.

CHAPTER 6

The Reformation
In Sweden

C HANGING THE COURSE OF A NATION often involves painful and bloody struggle for which the outcome is rarely predictable. No one in Sweden would have guessed that the Reformation of the Church which began in Germany with Martin Luther (1483-1546), would change the course of the whole nation.

The new teaching entered the Northern countries through three main channels, according to Prof. T. K. Derry: German preachers moving north, students who returned home from studies in Germany, and the Hanse merchants who spread their faith in foreign communities where they had business establishments. Besides that, the kings took an active part to set up a church under the protection and the control of the state.

Since the coming of Christianity to western and northern Europe, there had always been a strained relationship between kings and bishops. Both vied for power and control of the people and their wealth. Sweden became united with Denmark and Norway through the Union of Kalmar in 1397, largely through the superior military power of Denmark. The Swedes were unable to throw off the yoke of their Danish neighbors. Resistance movements, however, kept appearing and were crushed with force. In these political maneuvers, bishops took a strongly partisan role.

After an unsuccessful Swedish attempt at revolt led by Sten Sture, King Christian II of Denmark invaded Sweden with the backing of the Pope and Emperor Charles V. Sten Sture was killed and the local leaders were invited to a peace conference on November 7, 1520. They were assured that there would be full pardon for their resistance and that all would be forgotten. Once they were in control of the king, over one hundred of the patriots were executed, including two bishops, in what became known as the "Blood Bath of Stockholm." This was justified under the excuse that since they were also "heretics," they had no protection under the law. Before King Christian returned to Denmark, more than six hundred had lost their lives. The intention was to destroy the leadership of the resistance movements. The result, however, doomed Denmark's future in Sweden.

A young Swedish nobleman, Gustav Vasa, had been taken hostage to Denmark and imprisoned. Learning that his father had been one of the people massacred, Gustav escaped and made his way back to Sweden where he rallied the people and became king on June 6, 1523. He first invited the Pope to reform the church. The Pope demanded that Bishop Trolle, who had participated in the "Blood Bath," be restored to office. Gustav wouldn't agree to that because the bishop was pro-Danish. This led to the establishment of a Lutheran Swedish State Church over which the king was the head.

From earliest times there has been a close connection between the Scandinavian countries and Germany. When the Reformation of the Church broke out over the Indulgence Controversy at Wittenberg University in 1517, students of theology from Sweden were on hand to witness the events. Among these were Olavus Petri (1493-1552) and his brother Laurentius (1499-1573). They were born in Orebo, 150 miles west of Stockholm, sons of a blacksmith, and were educated at the Carmelite monastery near their home.

Olavus went for further study at the new university at Wittenberg in the spring of 1516. This was at the time when Martin Luther came into fame through writing his "Ninety-Five Theses" for debate on the eve of All Saints in 1517. Young Petri received a master's degree and returned to Sweden in November 1518 full of zeal for the Reformer's teachings. Having a degree from a German university was a matter of prestige in those days as it is today. Olavus was soon in great demand and it wasn't long before he became a teacher in the Cathedral School in Stockholm. In 1524, King Gustav Vasa appointed him to be secretary of the Stockholm City Council. Then the king commanded a pulpit to be put up in the Cathedral and authorized Olavus to preach sermons in Swedish. Sermons had not usually been a part of the worship service in the Middle Ages. The following year, Olavus put celibacy aside and was married.

Laurentius Petri also went to study in Wittenberg and returned to Sweden in 1527, after which he was appointed by the king to a professorship at Uppsala University. Four years later, Laurentius was elected archbishop of Uppsala, Sweden's most prestigious diocese, at age thirty-two. He presided over the office until 1573. One hundred and seventy priests took part in the election and the new archbishop received 150 of their votes votes.

This is where an interesting point in the Swedish church happened. The new bishop's consecration, which took place September 22, 1531, was performed by Petrus Magni, Bishop of Vasteras, who himself had been consecrated a bishop by Pope Clement VII in 1524. As a result, "Apostolic Succession" became a part of the Church of Sweden's tradition, unlike the churches of Denmark and Norway whose first evangelical bishops were consecrated by a professor of theology. "Apostolic Succession" means that there is a direct physical line of succession from the apostles to the bishops. While the Church of Sweden continues this tradition today, it places no special emphasis on it.

Olavus and Laurentius published the first Swedish Bible in 1541. Laurentius is especially remembered for his liturgical work. The Swedish church has a reputation for excellent music and liturgy, a tradition which was maintained in the former Augustana Lutheran Synod.

No one should think, however, that the Reformation issue was settled so simply in Sweden. After the death of Gustav Vasa in 1560, his heirs struggled over the country's religion. Even though Erik XIV (1560-1568) had Calvinistic leanings, he left the affairs of the church in the hands of Archbishop Petri. Erik's brother, John III (1568-1592) displayed sympathies for a "reformed Catholicism" and married a Polish princess.

John's son, Sigismund (1592-1599), reared in the Roman Catholic church, had become king of Poland in 1587. It was his intention to restore Sweden to obedience to Rome. Before he could lead his army over from Poland, his uncle, Duke Karl, entered the field with a military force to keep foreign influence out. In 1593, Karl called a convocation of the church which adopted the "Augsburg Confession" as the teaching of the

Swedish Church. *The Book of Concord,* which contains the historical writings of the Lutheran Church, was not officially adopted until 1663. Sigismund was defeated in 1598 and Karl IX became the ruler of Sweden. Anyone who rejected the Church of Sweden's teaching was in danger of banishment from the kingdom. Tolerance was not popular practice in those days. The Reformation in Sweden was completed through the reign of King Gustavus II Adolphus (1611-1632).

The Petri brothers are remembered by Swedes today with great respect. Erik Yelverton, an Anglican clergyman, has written: "Of all the Primates (Archbishops) who have occupied the See of Uppsala since its foundation in the twelfth century, none is more honoured in Sweden today for his achievements than Laurentius Petri of Neriki."

Today there is full freedom for all churches and religions in Sweden. If you ever visit Stockholm, be sure to see the Cathedral ("Storkyrkan") and the pulpit from which Laurentius Petri preached.

CHAPTER 7

Gustavus Adolphus –
'Lion Of The North'

WHO IS THE GREATEST SWEDE that ever lived? There have been many, but King Gustavus Adolphus (1594-1632) usually wins the popularity poll. Though only thirty-eight when he died, he changed Sweden from an isolated kingdom in the north to a modern nation respected by its neighbors. Rarely has one person shaped a nation so much.

My interest in famous people centers on their childhood influences. What made Gustavus such a dynamic leader? He was an exceptionally bright child and was trained from infancy to be a king. By age five, he had seen both battle and shipwreck and had learned to speak both Swedish and German. Under the guidance of a famous tutor, he studied literature, philosophy, theology, music, military science and gained skill in twelve languages. He was taught thrift and a strict moral code. His father, Charles IX, died when Gustavus was only seventeen, before the legal age to receive the crown. Axel Oxenstierna, one of the nobles, arranged for early accession. Before assuming power, he signed a charter of guarantees for the rights of the people. By sharing power, he gained more power.

Those were not good times. The political conflicts of Europe were deeply rooted in religious tensions. The "Thirty Years War" (1618-48) pitted Protestant against Roman Catholic. No war is good, but religious wars are the worst of all. Greed, jealousy and fear on both sides of the conflict has a way of turning theology into tragedy. Into such a struggle, the Swedish king came to the aid of the hard-pressed Protestant princes of Germany.

On June 17, 1630, Gustavus sailed with 13,000 men. Once in Germany, he was joined by an additional 26,000. What made him effective in battle was the superior training of his troops and the best artillery in Europe, plus mobility, discipline and a faster firing musket. But there was more. Each company of soldiers had its

21

own chaplain. There were prayers twice a day and a sermon once a week. Hymns were sung in battle. Gustavus led the only army in history to have no "camp followers." This kept them free from venereal disease. Another motivation to be successful was that unless they won, they didn't get paid.

On Nov. 6, 1632, Gustavus fell at Lutzen near Leipzig, while winning his last battle. His heart was wrapped in a silk shirt and returned to Sweden. Visitors may see the shirt in Stockholm today.

Important as the military victories of Gustavus are regarded, his domestic policies and administrative improvements were even more important. Sweden became one of the most efficient and well-organized governments in Europe. Oxenstierna guided the government while the king was away.

Gustavus Adolphus is honored in America by a college in St. Peter, MN, which was founded in 1862 and bears his name. His statue watches over the campus.

It is difficult for us who live today to judge the military heroes of the past. But there is no question how the contemporaries of Gustavus regarded him, even his enemies. They called him the "Lion of the North."

CHAPTER 8

The 'Great Northern War'

I NTERNATIONAL PROBLEM SOLVING is never simple. In the struggles of nations to achieve their "manifest destiny," there will always be conflict between what one nation perceives to be its destiny and what its neighbors suppose to be theirs. The result is often war.

When the Vasa family came to power in Sweden in the early 16th century, new energies were unloosed both in leadership and in the vision of their people. The most famous of the Vasa rulers, King Gustavus Adolphus (reigned 1594-1632), established Sweden's military power in Europe. Later Vasa kings also proved able leaders. As a result, Swedish military power became dominant in northern Europe by the time of Charles XII (reigned 1682-1718).

Because of Charles' aggressive foreign policies, a tide of resentment rose up against Sweden, especially in Denmark, but also in Poland, Saxony and Russia. At the same time, Russia came under the rule of Peter I, known as the "Great" (reigned 1672-1725). Peter was determined to obtain access for Russia to the great oceans for trade. He fought a war with Ottoman Turkey (1695-1696) for rights to the Black Sea. Only Sweden stood in his way to establish Russian access to the Baltic Sea. He also waged war against Persia to acquire access to the Caspian Sea (1722-1723).

Peter had acquainted himself with the ways of western Europe and travelled through those lands which were well advanced over Russia. He had an eye for a vast Russian empire, even employing the Danish sea Captain, Vitus Bering, to explore the ocean between Siberia and Alaska.

To prepare for his struggle with the Swedes, Peter concluded strategic alliances with Sweden's neighbors. In 1699, he made alliances with Denmark and Saxony. The ruler of Saxony was also the king of Poland. They were only too eager for the opportunity to challenge their warlike neighbor. The following year, the

Danish king, Christian V, attacked Holstein, an ally of Sweden. The Saxons moved against Livonia (Estonia and Latvia). Then after concluding a peace treaty with Turkey, Peter declared war on Sweden (1700).

This action resulted in the "Great Northern War" (1700-1721) which outlasted both kings. It is also called the "Second Northern War," the "First Northern War" being fought (1655-1660) between Sweden and Poland over succession rights to the Swedish throne. As a result, Poland gave up its claim to Swedish power and Sweden acquired Skane from Denmark.

It was a well coordinated attack. The Swedes, however, under the leadership of their energetic King Charles, and with the aid of the English and Dutch fleets, handed the Danes a swift defeat. The Saxon attack on Latvia was also broken and the Swedes defeated the Russians and their allies.

But then the tide of battle began to turn. Charles was moving in too many directions to encounter his enemy effectively. This gave them a chance to maneuver into better positions and be rested. Still the Russians and their allies feared to face Charles in battle unless they could have decided field advantage.

To establish his power more firmly in the North, Peter founded the city of St. Petersburg in 1703 as the seat of government (later called Leningrad: 1924-1991). He also built up a naval base at Kronstadt.

Charles suffered a series of defeats in Russia. The most decisive was at Poltava in June 1709. It had been his intention to capture Moscow. Like other invaders (Napoleon and Hitler), it ended in disaster. As a result, Charles fled to Turkey where he hoped to gain an ally based on anti-Russian policies. The Turks declared war on Russia in 1710, won a battle and then negotiated a truce. Angered, Charles issued a number of statements hostile to the Turkish government and his case began to fade.

Large countries like Russia always have a number of disaffected "minorities" who are looking for the opportunity to strike their own bargains. Of special interest was the promise that 20,000 Cossacks were ready to join Charles. This caught the Russians by surprise and stalled for time to regroup their forces. Unfortunately for Charles, only two thousand Cossacks showed up for battle and fled after a brief encounter.

Meanwhile, the anti-Swedish coalition started stripping away the Swedish empire in the Baltic. Charles was finally expelled from Turkey and he returned back to Sweden in November 1714 to try to save the situation. Other powers joined the coalition after the Swedish reversals. Both England and Hanover (northwest Germany) sided against Charles because he didn't honor his promises to give them territory in exchange for their neutrality in the war. Prussia entered the war against Charles in 1713, occupying nearby territories. Peter's diplomats were as effective as his armies, by signing treaties with Charles' enemies.

Charles met his end in southeastern Norway at the seige of Frederikshald in November 1718. There are some who said that he was shot in the back by one of his own officers who regarded him a tyrant. That's quite possible as there was a constant struggle in Sweden between the nobles and the king for control of the government.

Upon the death of Charles, his brother-in-law, Frederik, became king. Of German background and tired of Charles' policies, Frederik I of Sweden negotiated a series of peace treaties. The English recommended that Sweden sue for peace. Frederik took the advice and did quite well. Sweden, Saxony and Poland returned to their status before the war. Denmark returned its conquests to Sweden in exchange for a substantial amount of money. Sweden gave up claims to cities in Germany. The Treaty of Nystad was concluded on September 10, 1721. Russia got what it wanted, access to the Baltic Sea.

The "Great Northern War" was a turning point in the politics of northern Europe. Sweden began a decline in military power and Russia was on the ascent in the Baltic.

The Great Northern War was a decisive factor in the development of Russian military science and was the start of a regular Russian army, with infantry, cavalry and artillery. They also built up a naval fleet. Peter wisely calculated his political goals before taking military offensive. His goal was access to the ocean for trade. He never wavered from this goal and won. Russian armed forces adopted the most advanced European military tactics under Peter's leadership, especially using the bayonet charge under fire. Peter achieved success by learning from Sweden's military tactics and armament. Peter toured western lands – Prussia, Holland and England – to learn what he could in order to defeat Sweden and to gain his "window to the west."

If Charles had pursued an active foreign policy of negotiating with his neighbors, he might have defeated the Russians, because he was superior in the opening encounters. But because he did not "seek peace and pursue it" (the motto of the United States Air Force in 1988), he threatened his neighbors and they responded with an alliance against him.

Charles was the last of the real bellicose (warlike) Swedish kings. A tide of resistance began to successfully challenge the power of royalty. In another hundred years, Sweden joined the nations who became "peacemakers" and are still so today.

Of special interest to me is how polite and courteous the leaders of enemy nations can be to each other when signing peace treaties. If only they would hold a similar ceremony before the battles, perhaps many lives could be saved.

CHAPTER 9

Discovering
The 'Wasa Ship'

ONE OF THE MOST INTERESTING Scandinavian sites to visit is the Wasa Ship Museum in Stockholm. The "Wasa" was built in the days of Sweden's King Gustavus II Adolphus (1611-1632). He needed a navy to transport soldiers to the continent during the "Thirty Years War". For this he commissioned the building of the flagship "Wasa." It was to be the most magnificent warship on the Baltic Sea.

Henrik Hybertsson, one of the great Dutch shipbuilders of the time, was given the task of construction. Oak timbers were chosen which had the right curve. Each piece was checked against flaws. At two hundred feet in length and thirty-eight feet wide, it was a large vessel by the standards of its day. A thirty-foot bow jutted forward with a lion's head on the prow. It was a dizzy 170 feet to the top of the center sail. The "aftercastle" (top cabin) was sixty-five feet high. Four decks were built into the Wasa, two of them mounting sixty-four bronze cannons.

Over seven hundred carvings of saints and heroes adorned the vessel. No expense was spared for this Goliath of the sea. Just the appearance of such a floating fortress was intended to put terror into enemy sailors. The Wasa was to carry a crew of 135 plus three hundred soldiers.

On the beautiful Sunday afternoon of August 10, 1628, the Wasa took its maiden voyage from the royal castle through the canals out to sea. A number of women and children were allowed to ride as it passed through the city. The flagship was a magnificent sight, adorned in goldleaf and colorful pennants.

Suddenly, a powerful gust of wind hit the sails and the ship leaned hard to portside. Water gushed into the open ports. A few moments later, the proud ship went topside and sank in 110 feet of water. About fifty people perished.

What went wrong? The ship builder claimed that His Majesty had approved the plans. The Admiral had known of its instability, yet he did nothing about it. It was simply top-heavy. There was not enough ballast (weight) in the hold. If there had been, the first row of cannons would have been under water!

Some of the bronze cannons were retrieved with the use of a diving bell in the 1660s. But it took another three hundred years before a successful salvage took place. The Wasa was located in 1956. After a very delicate lifting operation, the Wasa broke surface on April 24, 1961. For many years the Wasa was housed in a temporary aluminum shelter. Today a new permanent building houses the warship and visitors may inspect it. In a nearby museum, some of the 25,000 recovered artifacts are on display: coins, pewter, pottery, furniture and other items.

The Wasa is housed in warm and humid air to preserve the wood. But even after 333 years under water, it bears a proud look. The wooden carvings remain impressive. Why? Because the tiny termite ("Teredo Navalis") which feeds on wooden wrecks, does not thrive in the low-salt waters of the Baltic Sea.

We don't know what would have happened to the fortunes of the Swedish king if the Wasa would have proved a worthy vessel. But one thing is certain. The grand ship would not be on display where visitors to Stockholm can see it today if it had not sunk.

CHAPTER 10

The Scandinavian 'Oscars'
And The 'French Connection'

EVERYONE KNOWS THAT AN "OSCAR" is an award for outstanding acting in the movies. Long before there was a Hollywood, two "Oscars" were kings of Sweden: Oscar I (1844-1859) and Oscar II (1872-1907). Actually, the Oscars of Sweden were not originally Swedes at all, but French. The stage for this change in Scandinavian politics came through the wars of Napoleon.

Denmark and Norway had shared the same rulers since Queen Margaret I in 1380, when the last "Norwegian" king of Norway died. The arrangement seemed eternal. This was made clear to me when I visited Surnadal, a community about seventy-five miles southwest of Trondheim. King Christian V (reigned 1670-1699) travelled from Copenhagen to that Norwegian valley in the summer of 1685. The king presented a plaque to the people which now hangs in the Mo Church. As an American whose paternal grandfather left there in 1892, I was surprised at the importance still attached to that "ancient" event. The point was that both Denmark and Norway seemed to believe that they would stay together forever.

The political destiny of my ancestral valley, however, was to change radically by new events taking place on the continent of Europe. Napoleon was on the march to conquer the world. Except for a bad winter in Russia, he might have succeeded. Napoleon ordered his marshall, Jean Baptiste Jules Bernadotte, to occupy Denmark if the Danes would not declare war on England. King Frederick VI (reigned 1808-1839) was immediately confronted with an English counter-threat. After weighing his unhappy choices, the Danish king cast his lot with Napoleon. He concluded that Denmark had more to fear from the French army than from the English navy. On April 12, 1801, Lord Nelson directed the British bombardment of Copenhagen. The Danish navy was destroyed and its merchant ships were taken to England as prizes of war. The Danes were never compensated. It also meant that

29

Norway was cut off from Denmark and suffered severely from a blockade.

Another surprise took place. Sweden's royal house of Vasa had run out of heirs. In searching about for new royalty, they elected Marshall Bernadotte as crown prince, to the pleasure of Napoleon. The French emperor privately disliked and feared the marshall and this was an opportunity to send him to Sweden. It could also provide him with an ally against England and Russia. Once in Sweden, Bernadotte switched sides. He joined the enemies of Napoleon. His reward was Norway. At the Treaty of Kiel, signed on January 14, 1814, Denmark gave up Norway to the Swedish king under threat from the "super-powers." It was to be Sweden's compensation for its loss of Finland to Russia just a few years before. The French marshall was secretly wishing for Napoleon's defeat and hoped that he would become the new king of France. He had accepted the Swedish offer with some private reservations. When that time came, however, the French chose their new king from the House of Bourbon. Bernadotte made a good choice since the Bourbons were kicked out of power in France in July 1830. It wasn't much longer before the French decided to be done with royalty altogether.

Bernadotte chose the name of Karl XVI Johan. English historians call him Charles John. The main street in Oslo leading from the palace to the parliament building is called "Karl Johansgate." He never did learn to speak Swedish, much less Norwegian. His son, Oscar I, and his grandson, Oscar II also served as kings of both Sweden and Norway. The Bernadottes are the royal family of Sweden today and Karl XVI Gustaf is dearly loved as a true Swede.

History ought to be read like a detective novel or a mystery story. One of the mysteries to me has been why so many Norwegian families named their sons "Oscar," since Norway had been forced into accepting a Swedish ruler by military threat. Besides, I'd heard some things as a young boy that Swedes and Norwegians were supposed to be "cool" towards each other. Why then did so many Norse immigrant families name their sons after King Oscar who lived in Stockholm?

I think I have found the answer. Oscar II was king of Sweden and Norway from 1872-1905, when he resigned the Norwegian throne. He lived two more years as the king of Sweden. That was the main emigrant period from Norway to America. He was a popular king in Norway and had been called the "Norwegian Prince." Immigrant families honored King Oscar naming their sons after him.

There may be another reason too. In my home community, almost every family had a son named "Oscar." I learned that a great many of these immigrants were from Trondelag, the area around Trondheim (it was called "Trondhjem" until 1930). Historian T. K. Derry has pointed out that many people in early migration into Trondelag had come by way of Sweden and there has always been a pro-Swedish sentiment in that part of Norway.

So one of the great mysteries of my childhood is now solved. I now know why my father was named "Oscar." If he ever knew the reason, he never told me. And I suspect that he lived his whole life quite unaware of the "French connection."

SWEDEN AND THE SWEDISH HERITAGE IN THE 'OLD WORLD'

CHAPTER 11

Fredrika Bremer – Early
Swedish Visitor To America

NOT EVERYONE WHO CAME FROM EUROPE to the New World intended to remain as an immigrant. There were many distinguished visitors who returned to tell their stories. Among the best known ones were Alexis de Tocqueville of France, Charles Dickens of England and Antonin Dvorak of Czechoslovakia (then under the Austro-Hungarian monarchy).

There were also many others from Russia, Japan, Argentine, Ireland, Liberia, Poland, Germany, Holland, Cuba, India, Italy, China and Scandinavia, just to mention a few. Among these was a delicate woman, Fredrika Bremer (1801-1865), who was born in Finland of a wealthy Swedish family. She showed an early aptitude for writing, publishing her first book in 1828.

The name Fredrika Bremer sounds more German than Swedish. Many German families of lower nobility and wealth moved to Scandinavia to work in government or in business. Many of them adopted their new homelands while retaining their names. The German community in Stockholm at one time had strong influence in government and even today there is a German section in the city with a German-speaking church.

Fredrika turned down an offer of marriage from a dear friend, claiming that her mission in life was to help the distressed, to further women's rights and to continue her writing career. Her domestic novels marked the beginning of the "realistic novel" in Sweden.

She was well informed of the world's great literature and was attracted to travel stories from the New World. It was quite the thing those days for young writers to go to America and to gain fame by publishing their stories upon return to Europe. Fredrika was especially influenced by Tocqueville's *Democracy in America*.

SWEDEN AND THE SWEDISH HERITAGE IN THE 'OLD WORLD'

In 1849, Fredrika went to America (first class!), the only Swede and one of a dozen women aboard the ship. While at sea, she read Longfellow's *Evangeline*. Arriving in New York, she was the guest at the Astor House and was feted with many parties. Her fame had preceded her arrival. Soon she met the best known American writers: George Bancroft, William Cullen Bryant, Washington Irving, Bayard Taylor and John Greenleaf Whittier. Whittier described her as the "Seeress of the misty Nordland, daughter of the Vikings bold."

She found the banquet trail in America to be quite overwhelming and wearisome. She wrote: "It was too much! And that is the way they kill strangers in this country." But for all that, she really liked America and developed a love affair with the land and people as the way of the future. Unlike Charles Dickens, she saw the good in this land and had no little influence on encouraging the large numbers of Swedish immigrants during the nineteenth century.

New England was regarded as the center of America to many European visitors. Fredrika was a guest of Ralph Waldo Emerson, Henry Wadsworth Longfellow and James Russell Lowell. She had respect for all of them but she regarded Emerson as the "Himalaya of heathenism." Her devout Christian piety did not mesh with the "Transcendentalism" of New England. She did admire Emerson, however, and was the first to translate his writings.

The institution of slavery in America was repulsive to most European visitors and Fredrika was no exception. She did not, however, side in with the radical abolitionists such as William Lloyd Garrison. She thought they were too violent in their tone of opposition. Many Scandinavians believed that slavery was doomed to die its own death.

She remained personally open to people of the South and was treated most generously there, despite her known anti-slavery views. After visiting one large plantation, she stated that she would rather live on bread and water than be a slave. She travelled through South Carolina, Georgia, Florida and even Cuba.

Unlike many visitors who remained in the East, Fredrika went west to Chicago, Wisconsin and Minnesota. Of Minnesota, she wrote: "This Minnesota is a glorious country, and just the country for Northern emigrants – just the country for a new Scandinavia." She called St. Paul "one of the youngest infants of the Great West." An elementary school in Minneapolis is named after her.

During her two-year stay in America, she travelled through twenty-seven of the thirty-one states by steamboat, train, stage-coach and covered wagon. On her way back to Sweden in the autumn of 1851, Fredrika visited some of the famous writers of England. Upon her return, she wrote a 650-page description of her trip entitled *The Homes of the New World: Impressions of America* (*Hemmen in den nya verlden*).

Her interest in women's rights was strengthened in America where girls studied foreign languages, mathematics and natural sciences, subjects thought to be too difficult for the female intellect in Sweden. She especially admired Harriet Beecher Stowe for writing *Uncle Tom's Cabin*. She wrote: "What will not that people become who can produce such daughters!" Back in Sweden, Fredrika devoted herself to social reform, welfare work and women's rights, much of which she had learned in America. Nathaniel Hawthorne visited with her in Rome and wrote: "She is the most amiable little woman, worthy to be the maiden aunt of the whole human race."

Though she did not remain as an immigrant, Fredrika loved America and her heart bled for her friends during the Civil War. She prayed for the reconciliation of the states and lived to see the end of hostilities. Her overall impression of America was that everyone here was in a hurry and was impatient with imperfection. She believed this was the reason for so much divorce in the New World.

Even today, visitors from Scandinavia and other countries look us over and make the same comments. However, they love America as a land moving into the future and not stuck in its past.

CHAPTER 12

Selma Lagerlof And
'The Adventures Of Nils'

I WENT INTO A BOOKSTORE across the street from the Sergel Plaza Hotel in Stockholm and asked: "What have you got by Selma Lagerlof?" Quickly the clerk pointed to *The Wonderful Adventures of Nils* and *The Further Adventures of Nils*, published in one volume. "This book," she said, "is very popular in Sweden today." I bought it.

Selma Lagerlof (1858-1940) was the first woman and the first Swedish writer to be given the Nobel Prize for Literature. She was born in Varmland, a beautiful area through which the Oslo to Stockholm train travels. As a small child she was not able to walk alone. When other young people were off to parties, dancing and having a good time, Selma would stay home with her grandmother who told her the stories of old Sweden while knitting. Lameness, however, did not prevent her imagination from entering into the stories. Selma imagined herself to be matching wits with ferocious wolves and attacking bears. Elves, gnomes and ghosts were all part of the nights she spent in a dark attic room.

Selma's energies turned to writing. Her diary, written at age fifteen, describes a trip to Stockholm for medical care. Her family was acquainted with many of the leading citizens of Sweden. This enriched her awareness of the times. But Selma also knew poverty. "Marbacka," the estate where she had grown up had to be sold. After teaching a number of years and becoming a successful writer, she bought it back.

Two books established her fame: "Gosta Berlings Saga" (1891) and the story about Nils Holgersson (1906). Nils was a mischevous fourteen-year-old who delighted in tormenting the farm animals. One Sunday, he refused to go to church with his parents. Ordered to read the Scriptures for the day and Luther's Sermon on the text, he promptly fell asleep. Waking, he saw an elf looking into his mother's trunk. He captured the tiny creature but was transformed into the size of an elf himself. The animals now had their turn to torment him.

A flock of wild geese flew over and called to the huge gander on the Holgersson farm to join them. Knowing what a loss that would be to his parents, Nils grabbed the gander around its neck. In the next moment, Nils was on the gander's back, flying the length and breadth of the land. Legends and fairy tales are woven into the story which relates Swedish geography and history. The author's moral optimism won the day. Nils returned to his parents as a humbled, grateful and obedient son. He became a full-sized human again. In the meantime, he experienced a series of scary escapades. He spoke the language of the animals and they became his teachers.

Nils was rescued by the author from an owl at Marbacka, when she returned to visit her ancestral home. That is how she learned his story. The adventures of Nils is entertaining reading for both children and adults. In a time when the risque, the sexually explicit and sadism are considered necessary for a writer's success, to find good writing done in wholesome expressions is like finding the pearl of great price.

Dalarnahest, a Swedish horse.

CHAPTER 13

Prince Eugen's Island

EVERYONE HAS A DAY THAT IS REMEMBERED with some special nostalgia. One of the most delightful days I have spent was in Stockholm on a Sunday afternoon in August. The sunshine was beautiful and the temperature was perfect. Together my wife and I strolled from the Sergel Plaza Hotel to the waterfront. We looked at statues in the parks, including one of the famous inventor, John Ericsson, who designed the U.S. Monitor of Civil War fame. Then we took a ride on a motor launch through the canals. It is these waterways that have given Stockholm the name "Venice of the North."

We docked in front of the royal palace when the changing of the guard was taking place. These honorary guards all looked seven feet tall in their uniforms. There were hundreds of sailboats and motor launches out that afternoon. A couple of stops later, we got off the boat at Waldemarsudde, popularly known as "Prince Eugen's Island." It's a natural paradise. There are magnificent flower gardens, statues, a museum and a view of Stockholm that is unequalled.

We found a park bench in the shade overlooking the harbor and ate our picnic lunch. Across the canal was an ocean liner loading for the sixteen-hour trip to Helsinki, Finland. Time limitations ruled out that ride for us on this trip. It was to come a year later. The panorama included castles, church spires, department stores and miles of harbors and shoreline. There was just enough wind to move the sailboats along at a good speed in and out of the paths traversed by motorized boats.

My curiosity, however, got the best of me. Who was this Prince Eugen (1865-1947)? What was the story behind the stately castle and the museum on this island? And why was it named after him? He was the youngest son of Oscar II, who was King of Sweden from 1872-1907. Having no expectation of royal succession, Prince Eugen became a great artist and a collector of art.

One has to try to have some feeling for a prince who can never hope to become king. What should he do? To appreciate Prince Eugen, you also need to get acquainted with his talented and industrious friends, many of whom became quite famous. There were an unusual number of noted Swedish artists and writers at that time. Their pattern was to go to the Continent, especially France, to study. They were often given financial support by the government for their studies. These artists were deeply in love with their native land.

Among them were Carl Larsson, Bruno Liljeforst, Gustav Fjaestad and Anders Zorn. Another brilliant artist of the times was Carl Milles, famous for his sculptures. One of these, called "Meeting of the Waters," is on Market Street in front of the historic St. Louis train depot. It pictures the meeting of the Missouri and Mississippi rivers.

After considerable time in Germany, Austria and France, Prince Eugen returned to Sweden where he became famous for his artistic skills. He was very popular and greatly loved by everybody in the country. I learned a lot from this boat ride and will always be ready for the next one.

CHAPTER 14

Skansen –
Sweden In Miniature

I F YOU COULD VISIT JUST ONE PLACE IN SWEDEN, where would you go? I'd suggest Skansen, an open-air museum which covers seventy-five acres. Two million people a year visit Stockholm's greatest tourist attraction, twice as many people as live in Sweden's capital city.

Back in 1891 when Skansen was founded, it was on the outskirts of the city, but today it's a green and car-free oasis in the middle of the city. You get a magnificent view on all sides. The skyline is marked by copper roofs, church steeples, Sergels Tower and modern skyscrapers, plus the hills and canals.

Skansen has a little bit of every part of Sweden. It is arranged with a feeling for geography. For example, the Lapp village is placed in the northwest. The far northern part is ringed with natural habitat for the larger wild animals. Moose, bears, wolves, wolverines, lynx and even European Bison, now extinct except in captivity, live peacefully in the heart of this beautiful metropolitan area. Most of the animals are native to Sweden, but since this is Stockholm's only zoo, there are also some tropical exhibits.

Skansen was the dream of Arthur Hazelius who began collecting Swedish cultural exhibits in 1872. A practical man with an eye for education, he wanted to preserve some of the everyday life from Sweden's past. He seemed to sense that the twentieth century would bring sweeping changes to his country.

With meticulous effort, Hazelius brought buildings and furnishings to Stockholm. His work has served as a model for other open-air museums throughout the world. Of special interests are the farmsteads transplanted into Skansen. In the earlier days when people could not drive to town for all of their needs, the blacksmithing, baking, cloth making and sewing had to be done on the farm. It took many buildings. The farm owners lived in the main house and the workers in others. Cattle were housed in buildings which joined the living quarters of people.

Of special interest is the summer farmstead, the "faabod," called "seter" in Norway. These were usually found in northern Sweden and were places where cattle, goats and sheep were kept in the summer. Sometimes there was a nearby summer farm and another up to fifty miles away from home. Usually these summer farms were jointly owned by eight to ten families with about twenty-five cows. They were tended for about nine weeks in the summer by older women with the help of children. They also put up hay, and made cheese and butter.

I found only one building in Skansen that was imported. It was a "stabbur" from Telemark in Norway. The Swedes also used these houses to store dairy products and food. There is also a large "Dalarnahest" (a horse carved from wood in Dalarna) with steps for people to climb up on and have their picture taken. To have your picture taken on it is a child's equivalent of being photographed on a camel near the pyramids at Gizeh in Egypt.

Skanson is both an historical museum and a recreational center. There are restaurants, theatres, art exhibits and concerts. Skansen is ten times as large today as it was in 1891. The exhibits and animal habitats are constantly being improved. I spent several hours walking through it with a guide book. If you go to Stockholm, insist on visiting Skansen. It's Sweden in miniature.

Spinning wheel demonstrated at Skanson.

CHAPTER 15

Carl Milles –
Swedish Artistic Genius

MY FIRST ENCOUNTER WITH CARL MILLES (1875-1955) was when we moved to St. Louis in 1961. I used to travel a good deal by railroad in those days. Out in front of the old St. Louis Train Depot is a large set of sculptures called "Meeting of the Waters." It was completed by Milles in 1940.

It's a grandiose display of fourteen bronze sculptures with water spouting and spraying. The fountains symbolize the coming together of the Missouri and Mississippi rivers just north of the city. Whenever I visit the home town of Cardinal baseball, I like to take another look at this famous work of art. It's located on Market Street about a half mile west of Busch Stadium and the famed Gateway Arch. Today the old train depot has been converted into a classy shopping mall, but Milles' work of art stands as grand as ever.

One of the questions that goes through my mind when I read of people who turn out to be winners is about their early years of life. How did they get started on the road to success? Milles was born near Uppsala, Sweden. It's an historic and cultural area of the country. At age seventeen, he became apprenticed to a cabinet maker in Stockholm and attended a technical school. Four years later Milles took off for Paris to study art under the famous Auguste Rodin, well known in the school of Impressionism. He remained in Paris for eight years.

Milles was so engrossed in his study of sculpturing that he got a lung inflammation from breathing stone dust. It bothered him for the rest of his life. By 1908 he was well enough to return to Sweden and settled in the suburb of Lidingo in Stockholm. There he built a studio called "Millesgarten."

In 1920, Milles became a professor at the Swedish Royal Academy. It wasn't long, however, before he found this too confining and returned to his studio. In 1931, he was invited to be the head of the department of sculpture at Cranbrook Academy of Art in Bloomfield Hills, Michigan. Now he made his name in America as well as in Europe. In 1945, Milles became an American citizen and turned over the management of his beloved "Millesgarten" to a private institution. During the winters of 1950-55, he was at the American Academy in Rome. He died at the age of eighty in his native Sweden.

Two famous teachers left their mark on Milles. Rodin, the impressionist from Paris and the German sculptor-theorist, Adolf von Hildebrand, who helped him to blend classical art forms (Greek and Roman) with the Nordic goblins and trolls.

Milles, however, developed his own special style. He had a flair for charming decorative effects. Among his well known works are "Europa and the Bull" in Halmstad, Sweden. He did one of Sten Sture, the popular Swedish patriot. The "Folkunga Fountain" in Linkoping, Sweden, pictures a rider on a wild steed. There are twenty of his sculptures in Stockholm alone. That's how much the Swedes think of him.

I am not an artist or a student of art. But I've learned a lot from artists and my appreciation of them grows with years. If you go to St. Louis, be sure to see the "Meeting of the Waters" and remember Carl Milles, Sweden's artistic genius. Better still, go to Stockholm and see "Millesgarten." The Swedes will love you for just asking to visit their favorite sculptor's art treasures.

*Millesgarten
in Stockholm.*

CHAPTER 16

Alfred Nobel
And The 'Prizes'

I F YOU TAKE A TOUR OF STOCKHOLM, your guide will certainly point out the Grand Hotel and comment, "that's where the Nobel prizes are announced." The awards in physics, chemistry, medicine and literature have been given there since 1901. The award for economics, given only since 1969, is also announced in Stockholm. The politically important Nobel Peace Prize is given out in Oslo.

The man who started the world's most prestigious awards was Alfred Nobel (1833-1896), a Swedish chemist. Nobel's father had been an inventor and made it possible for him to study in St. Petersburg and in the United States. His international fame came from experimenting with nitroglycerin in his father's factory. In 1867, after years of work, he combined it with an absorbent substance that could be safely shipped. He called it "dynamite," from a Greek work meaning "power." Nobel intended it to be used for peaceful purposes, especially in engineering and in road building.

It wasn't long before Nobel became one of the richest men in the world. He built factories in many countries and purchased the Bofors armament plant in Sweden. Among the other things he experimented on were synthetic rubber and artificial silk. A lover of literature, he wrote several plays and novels. These, however, did not bring him fame.

An idealistic Swede, Nobel's fragile health suffered intense guilt when he saw his prized dynamite being used for war. He had only thought of peace. In his will, an endowment fund of nine million dollars, money from his estate, was set aside for prizes to promote international peace. The value of each prize had reached $180,000 by 1981. The Swedish Central Bank provides the money for the economics prize.

All the awards except the Peace Prize are given out in Stockholm. But for some unclear reason, Nobel turned over the management of this award to the Norwegian Storting

(Parliament) which appoints a committee of five to make its selection. All the awards are made on December 10, the anniversary of Nobel's death. Two or more persons may share the prize, or no award may be made at all. No one is allowed to apply for these prizes. Nominations must be made by a "qualified" person.

Immense prestige is connected with the Nobel prizes in addition to the money. I noted this on a trip to Scandinavia in 1985 when I obtained a copy of the Yearbook for the Norwegian State Church. The picture of Bishop Desmond Tutu of South Africa was on the front cover. In the American press, hardly a reference is made to the Bishop without noting that he is a "Nobel Peace Prize" winner. The award reflects the feelings of the Scandinavian people. They have been among the strongest to oppose the Apartheid policies of the South African government and the Scandinavian Air System stopped flights to South Africa on this account. The Nobel recognition of Bishop Tuto has added to his stature as a leader in his country.

To read through the list of awards since they began in 1901 is to review a "who's who" of the world's most influential people in the twentieth century. Besides Bishop Tuto, some of the other award winners have been Wilhelm Roentgen, Theodore Roosevelt, Rudyard Kippling, Albert Einstein, Selma Lagerlof, George Bernard Shaw, Niels Bohr, Arthur Compton, Jane Addams, Enrico Fermi, Linus Pauling, Winston Churchill, Dag Hammarskjold, Albert Schweitzer, Milton Friedman, Norman Borlaug, Elli Wiesel and Mother Theresa. Americans have won the largest number of awards, followed by the Germans, English and French. Seven organizations have won awards, including the United Nations High Commission of Refugees. Only two winners have declined to accept, Boris Pasternak (1973) and Jean Paul Sartre (1977), both in literature.

It's a strange twist of events that the Scandinavians, once the terror of western Europe, should now be the world's foremost promoters of peace; and that the invention of dynamite, intended for peace, should now be the stock in trade for terrorists. The nine million dollar trust fund still speaks eloquently in a time when the money of "influence" is counted rather in the billions.

CHAPTER 17

Carl Larsson's Home

I T'S A "MIRACLE" how a talented artist can take what is plain and ordinary, and transform it into a thing of exquisite beauty. Carl Larsson (1853-1919) was such an artist. Carl and his wife Karin took a small house "laying bare on a heap of slag" and turned it into one of the best known and most beloved homes in Sweden, if not "of all times," according to Ulf Hard, author of *Carl Larsson's Home.*

It was in 1889, when migrations to the New World from Sweden were claiming most of the country's attention, that Larssons moved into a house which they named "Little Hyttnas" (cottage) in the village of Sundborn in the province of Dalarna in the central part of the country. The house was a gift from Karin's father. It had just two rooms, an attic and an attached woodshed. Over the next two decades many rooms were added, and it still has not lost its quaint appearance of comfort and warmth, but no one would have recognized it.

Nineteenth century Sweden was an underdeveloped country and its capital, Stockholm, was a relatively small city with many poor neighborhoods. It's a wonder that a boy born in Gamla Stan (Old Town) should become the outstanding representative of the "new art." I've visited the community twice. Today it's a model of cleanliness and beauty. The old buildings have been renovated in magnificent style.

Carl's father has been described as a "ne'er-do-well" who abandoned his wife and family when Carl was a small child. His mother supported the family by washing and ironing. They were forced to move into a slum-section in the East End of Stockholm. Things were so bad that Larsson wrote: "If I say that the people who lived in these houses were swine I am doing those animals an injustice. Misery, filth and vice – every kind of vice flourished there – seethed and smouldered cozily; they were corroded and rotten, body and soul." He later wrote that he could remember nothing of happiness from his childhood. No wonder that he loved the peaceful woods of Dalarna.

When only thirteen, Larsson was encouraged by his teacher in the "poor school" to apply to the school where his maternal grandfather had studied art. Because of his background in poverty, he was shy and handicapped by an inferiority complex. After about three years, his shyness wore off and his artistic ability began to blossom. It was when he was editor of the school paper that his talent was discovered. He was hired by a humor magazine to draw cartoons. It wasn't long before he was earning a respectable salary. Then he supported his mother and a younger brother who was also artistically talented.

It wasn't long before Carl was travelling all over Sweden and even abroad as a sketching reporter. It soon became noted that wherever anything of importance happened, two people could be counted on to be present, Larsson and King Oscar II. When one of the students who had been a great inspiration to Larsson in Sweden died in 1877, he went to Paris with a heavy heart. Going to France was the fashionable thing to do for art students in those days. France was in low morale too, having been disastrously defeated by Germany in the war of 1870-1871. Larsson travelled to France several times before finding his niche. On one of his return trips to Sweden he did art illustrations for August Strindberg, a famous playwright.

Larsson continued to be afflicted with depression. A turning point in his life seems to have been when he made new friends at Gretz-Armain-villiers, a village outside of Paris where Scandinavians used to get together. He also made the acquaintance of some of Sweden's finest future artists there. Grez was a quaint village "full of charm," with an ancient arched bridge, a medieval church with moss-covered walls, and the ruins of a castle. Stone walls in front of houses, gardens with flights of stone steps and trellises with grape vines, plus fruit trees, made the village an artist's paradise.

It was at Gretz that Carl met Karin Bergoo, who had come from a well-to-do Swedish home with a liberal outlook on life, evidenced by the fact that she was allowed to be educated as an artist. They were married in 1883.

Larsson described the site of their house in Sundborn as having just a few small birch trees and some lilacs, plus a potato patch. Having limited means, they improved it by putting away extra savings whenever they could. With the help of some village carpenters, a blacksmith, a bricklayer and a painter, they put together a house which has become part of Sweden's pride. At first, it was just a summer house, but eventually, it became their permanent home. Today it is known as "Carl Larsson's Home" and has become a noted tourist attraction.

Carl and Karin were internationally oriented, but retained their romantic views of Sweden. Besides Paris, Carl had also gained artistic impressions in Berlin, Vienna and London. While Carl became famous as a painter, Karin gained her fame for weaving and embroidery.

The rooms in the Carl Larsson home look small to visitors today, but Larsson's painting had the effect of making them look larger than they were. Simplicity marked the interior planning. The main additions to the original log house began in 1890. It included an art studio with pictures to the front, and a large fireplace which added elegance. By 1900, more space was needed for the studio, so the original one was turned into a family room where Karin could do her work while the children did woodwork or played.

Sundborn became their permanent home in 1901. The woodshed was torn down and a two-story addition was added to make room for eleven persons. In 1912, a cottage was attached to the studio for the display of paintings. Author Ulf Hard claims that their home "became unique and exemplary and has so remained" as "a vital part of the culture at the turn of the century." Since 1943, the buildings have been administered by a family society. Above the door there is a wood carving, commonly done in Scandinavia, which reads: "Welcome to this house, to Carl Larsson and his spouse."

We're fortunate to have several books on Carl Larsson. In addition to the one on his house, he wrote six others. The best known are *Carl Larsson - On the Sunny Side* (1910) and *The World of Carl Larsson. On the Sunny Side* contains pictures of his paintings of the rooms in the house, about the children. Flowers were everywhere in the home. It reads as an autobiography and a story of life in the home. I have never run across anything quite so charming. *The World of Carl Larsson* deals with his art works, which are displayed in museums around the world.

I'm always amazed at human potential popping up in unexpected places. Here was a poor boy who became Sweden's greatest painter and illustrator of all time and has been acclaimed internationally. Known as the "sunshine man," Larsson occupies a place in Swedish consciousness which is shared by no other artist.

Carl Larsson

CHAPTER 18

The Movies Of
Ingmar Bergman

ERNEST INGMAR BERGMAN was born July 14, 1918, in Uppsala, Sweden. His father was a Lutheran pastor who became chaplain to the royal family. Reared in strict discipline which included corporal punishment and isolation, Bergman found his escape in movies. He saw his first movie at age six.

While staying at his grandmother's house in Dalarna, Bergman became acquainted with the projectionist at the local theatre. He was allowed to sit alongside of the projector and watch movies. When only nine years old, young Ingmar obtained a magic lantern and projected light on cut-outs which cast shadows on a screen. He'd do his own narrating while his young sister was a captive audience.

At nineteen, Ingmar entered the University of Stockholm to study art history and literature, and there he directed a campus drama group. After a bitter argument with his parents, he left the parsonage home, dropped out of school, and went to work as an errand boy at the Royal Opera House. At age twenty-four, he got a job with the Swedish Film Industry (Svensk Filmindustri) which today produces his movies.

Bergman did so well that he won the Grand Prix at the Cannes Film Festival in France in 1946. This is the world's most famous place for reviewing movies. If the Cannes critics give a good rating, it usually assures a success at the box office. Not all his early movies went so well, but he made his mark on the industry and worked harder than ever to make good.

The early Bergman movies were black and white. "Smiles of a Summer Night" won the prize for "Most Poetic Humor" at Cannes in 1956. It's the story about a Swedish lawyer and his mixed up love life. His son was a theology student preparing for the ministry who became quite confused between his concern for virtue and his father's libertine life. It's a genuine soap opera with

51

a far more interesting plot than you'll find on TV. It was a satirical spoof on the morals and social conventions of his day.

The following year Bergman made it big in Cannes again with "The Seventh Seal." The title, taken from the Apocalypse of St. John (Revelation 8), is an allegory on man's relation to God and how he tries to cope with death. Max von Sydow played the part of a knight recently returned from the Crusades in the Middle East. Having participated in that terrible debacle of death and destruction, he returned to Sweden in search for the meaning of life. Throughout the play, the knight plays chess with the devil for his life. Only after the devil, in the disguise of a priest during confession, prodded him to reveal his secret for winning, did he lose. The central theme is the dichotomy between God in his silence, appearing to be our enemy, and yet self-proclaimed as the creator and lover of life.

Since it was the Middle Ages, everything had to do with religion. Will Durant described that time as "the age of faith." The real struggle was for faith. The knight wants the devil to tell him what God may have told him about faith. As usual, the devil lied and he learned nothing. Several scenarios go on simultaneously: The burning of a young girl as a witch, shades of Salem in New England; "flagellants" preaching doom and the end of the world while administering torture to themselves as a way of atoning for their sins; and a travelling actor who got into all kinds of trouble because of religious visions. The movie has a contemporary psychoanalytic twist.

"Wild Strawberries" (1957) is built around a sequence of dreams filled with death tones by an octogenarian who has flashbacks. The elderly professor travels to Lund, an ancient university city in southern Sweden, to receive an honorary doctorate. This movie won first prize at the Berlin International Film Festival in 1958. In America "Wild Strawberries" was named the best foreign film in 1959 by the National Board of review. Bergman also received an Academy Award nomination in the category of best story and screenplay. The Oscar, however, went to Doris Day and Rock Hudson for their performance of "Pillow Talk."

Bergman's "The Magician" also reached America in 1959, again starring Max von Sydow. It's the story of a magician who, pretending to be mute, fooled everyone about his identity. After several scrapes with the law, he ended up doing a performance at the palace in Stockholm. Several critics have wondered if this movie was really Bergman's own spiritual autobiography. There are parallels to it in the Passion Play.

"The Virgin Spring," starring Max von Sydow, made the deepest impression on me of any of the Bergman movies I have seen. Set in the piety of the Middle Ages in Sweden, it portrays beautiful country scenes. It has been called his "masterwork," the most lyrical, compassionate and lucid of all his productions. It's heavy stuff and will probably raise your blood pressure and temperature. I don't recommend it for weak hearts. But I've seen nothing which I think better portrays life in medieval Scandinavia. In 1960 it was honored as the best foreign film at the Oscar awards in Hollywood.

These are some of the early Bergman films, all in black and white and all in Swedish. However, the English sub-titles are adequate and if you have some knowledge of any Scandinavian language, you will understand quite a bit of the narrative. Bergman emphasizes acting rather than words in his serious movies. The background music is worth listening to even if you didn't watch the movie. The more recent Bergman movies are in color as well as in English. The best way to see them, especially the older ones, is to find a video shop that has a foreign film section. In the larger cities, you may find Bergman's movies at a theatre.

In 1976, while rehearsing a new production of Strindberg's "Dance of Death" in Stockholm, Bergman was arrested and charged with tax fraud. It took two months before the authorities were satisfied that he was innocent. He was so offended by this experience that he left Sweden to settle in Munich, not returning until December 1977 to accept the Swedish Academy of Letter's "Great Gold Medal." Only seventeen people have received the award during the twentieth century. The following year he resumed the directorship of the Stockholm Royal Dramatic Theatre. Sweden was grateful for his return and established a prize for excellence in filmmaking to honor him.

Bergman's movies are not for everyone. He's both a showman and a moralist, both comic and serious. One critic describes him as a "filmmaker of magic with an evangelical point of view – a Druid captured by Lutheranism." Watching his movies requires thinking and reflection. You won't get bored and need popcorn to stay awake. If you have rigid Victorian manners, you may be offended and find it difficult to watch. But if you can stand it, the plot of these movies will linger in your consciousness for some time. They may even appear in your dreams. I'm looking forward to more of his productions. Bergman's autobiography, *The Magic Lantern* (Viking Press, 1988), will fill you in on the other interesting details of his life.

Ingmar Bergman

CHAPTER 19

August Strindberg –
Swedish Playwright

Y OU CAN NEVER ACCURATELY PREDICT the future of any child. This is one of the exciting things about life. Whenever I read a biography, I am less interested in a person's achievements than in the childhood experiences which influenced the direction of a person's life. August Strindberg (1849-1912) is a case in point.

Strindberg was born in Stockholm when its population was just ninety thousand. Today it has over 1,500,000 in its metropolitan area. It was a time of change and upheaval. Though his family had been normally well off financially, August was born when money was scarce in the wake of financial reverses. This left a deep mark on his soul. But it also challenged him to achieve.

Strindberg's early life was marked with a great deal of repression and the feeling that he was not loved. Because his two older brothers developed faster and handsomer than August, his parents favored them over him.

At age seven, he was sent off to the Klara school in Stockholm, known for its strictness. It was a long walk from his home, especially in the dark days of winter. He later wrote: "Facts were crammed in by means of the cane and by the fear of it." At age eleven, he persuaded his father to send him to the nearby Jakob school, a place where most of the children came from poorer families. August liked this school well and forever became attached to those people.

When August was only thirteen, his mother died. While he never did feel fully approved by his mother, at least she was a way he could communicate with his father. Shortly afterwards, his father married the governess who was thirty years younger than himself, and just barely older than his oldest son. This caused more problems for young August as she was always resorting to pietism and puritanism to get her way. August rebelled against this repressive and suffocating religion. It showed in his writings for the rest of his life.

Young August, however, was a religious person. At age seventeen, he gave a sermon in church. He was very proud of his accomplishment but stated that he hated the regalia he had to wear when giving it, especially the stiff, ruffled collar.

At age eighteen, Strindberg went off to Uppsala University, north of Stockholm. He dropped out after a year and then went back for two more years. He left, however, without getting a degree. At the University he concentrated on sciences, especially chemistry. But his main interest was in the theatre. He wrote seventy-five plays, thirteen works of fiction and nineteen other books, some in more than one volume.

Strindberg is most famous for his plays. Some of these have been made into movies. In a Stockholm hotel room, I watched one of his plays on television. It was an exciting part of being in Sweden. His movies are hard to find in America, but you might inquire at a video shop. While regarded as a serious writer, he could also excel in humor.

It's always interesting to learn what the folks back home think of a local person who has become an international celebrity. In Sweden, Strindberg was not only looked upon as a dramatist and a writer, but as a political figure, publicly controversial and anti-establishment. His older brother wrote that August was always trying to convince others that there were two sides to every issue. Then he'd try to persuade you about his way.

The Germans gave Strindberg a hero's welcome. They looked on him as having a religious calling to expose materialistic corruption. By the time of his death (1912), there were two hundred editions of his writings in German. His plays were hailed as the drama of the human soul. He disagreed with Freud's sexual understanding of life, but this may have been partly because he had trouble with his own sexuality. He looked for a higher (transcendental) reason to interpret life. His writings also coincided with the "expressionist" views of the times. The Germans regarded him as the poet of the middle classes.

By contrast, Strindberg found little support among the French, likely because of his popularity in Germany. Neither did he have much success in America or in England. This may have been in part because of the great popularity that Norway's Henrik Ibsen held in these places. These two famous dramatists differed especially in one area: Feminism. While Ibsen had been "enshrined as the saint of the feminists and liberals," Strindberg vehemently opposed the feminist movement as "an aristocratic movement, a political upper-class movement, in which women were employed as agitators," according to Spinchorn in his book *Strindberg as Dramatist*. Strindberg warned women that this would eventually lead to a new slavery for them. He claimed that a change on women's social position would lead to a damaging political upheaval. Strindberg's own experience with women was anything but happy, starting with his mother and step-mother. He was married and divorced three times.

Strindberg was controversial because he tried to write about the world from a different point of view than was popular. He may have been misunderstood because people judged all of him for what was really just a part, or a phase of him.

He shared Albert Einstein's theory of "relativity" with regard to life. While most writers of the time held to a "solid state" view of the world, Strindberg believed that everything is constantly changing. Einstein stated: "Body and soul are not two different things, but only two different ways of perceiving the same thing." Strindberg wrote: "Life would be pretty monotonous if one thought and said the same things all the time." He could also laugh at his own past work.

Strindberg's life was tragic from some points of view, but he worked hard to improve his skills. He would study dictionaries, read books on grammar and wrestle with linguistic studies. Curiously, he held that Hebrew was the original language of the world. So did my Hebrew professor in college.

He summarized his own life saying: "Thought about my life this way: Is it possible that all these terrible things I have experienced were especially staged for me, so that I could become a playwright, capable of describing all manner of psychic conditions and situations? I was a playwright at age twenty, but if my life had proceeded in a calm and orderly fashion, I would not have had anything to render into drama."

On approaching death, he gave specific instructions for his funeral. One of these was to place a crucifix on his chest when he died. His gravestone bore this epithet (in Latin) "O Cross, Be Greeted, Our Only Hope."

The funeral was meant to be a private ceremony at eight o'clock in the morning. The day of burial turned out to be a Sunday and thousands came to honor him, both from Sweden and foreign countries. Especially noticeable in attendance because of their red banners, were the laboring people of Stockholm, for whom he had become a hero. The funeral liturgy was conducted by Archbishop Nathan Soderblom, head of the Swedish State Church.

Strindberg makes you think. That's a lost art in most of the entertainment media of today. I have another interest in Strindberg. His grandfather was a pastor. I'm always curious about how pastors' grandchildren turn out.

August Strindberg

CHAPTER 20

Raoul Wallenberg –
'Righteous Gentile'

RAOUL WALLENBERG is the most famous "missing person" in the world. There's been a million dollar reward for his safe return to freedom. Very few people knew his fate, but most westerners didn't believe their explanations.

The Wallenbergs are a respected Swedish family, distinguished as statesmen, diplomats and bankers. Raoul was born August 4, 1912, into a less wealthy branch of the family. His father, a naval officer, died three months before his birth. Fortunately, he had a strong-hearted mother.

After graduating with distinction in architecture from the University of Michigan in 1935, Raoul tried banking in South Africa and Palestine. He found it to be "too calm, cynical and cold." Architecture was his dream, though he went into international trade. The family thought his talents were in politics.

While in Palestine, Wallenberg came in contact with Jewish refugees from Germany. He was moved by their persecution and by the anti-semitism which he found. It touched him more deeply because his great-great grandfather, Michael Benedicks, was a German Jew.

During World War II, the evidence was mounting that most European Jews were being destroyed by Hitler. Adolf Eichmann, a heartless sadist, came to Hungary in March 1944 to personally exterminate the country's Jewish population. His cunning and cruelty knew no bounds. The Allied powers were slow to respond with help. But finally, President Roosevelt gave his support to save them through the United States War Refugee Board.

Strange as it may seem, it finally came down to one man, thirty-one-year-old Raoul Wallenberg. He joined the Swedish legation in Budapest and assembled 250 Jewish volunteers who were given Swedish diplomatic protection. He rented thirty-two houses over which he flew the Swedish flag to shelter fifteen Jews and set up two hospitals, soup kitchens and a children's home. Portuguese, Swiss and Vatican legations also gave help. Surviving many Nazi attempts to kill him, it is believed that he saved over 100,000 Jews of Budapest by giving them "protective passes." Bribery and threats of post-war punishment were his weapons against the Nazis.

On January 17, 1945, as the Russian army approached, Wallenberg was summoned to the Soviet military headquarters. Though warned against going, he went in hopes of negotiating with them on behalf of the Jewish people. Soviet paranoia and treachery, however, regarded him as a danger to their rule. That was his last day of freedom.

Until late 1987, there was hope that Wallenberg was still alive. Then the Kremlin advised his family that he died of a heart attack in a Soviet prison in 1947. Despite this report which has been accepted by his family as factual, there are former Soviet prisoners who have returned to the West who claimed they had seen him and spoken to him since that time. The new Russian republic is reported to have recently turned his file over to his family.

The government of Israel has declared Wallenberg a "Righteous Gentile." The United States government has made him an "honorary citizen." He is only one of three foreign nationals ever to be granted such a recognition. As a part of the "New Sweden '88" celebration, Gustavus Adolphus College had a special lecture on Wallenberg by Ambassador Per Anger who had been a personal friend and colleague of Wallenberg.

A tree has been planted in his honor at Yad Vashem, Israel's memorial to the Holocaust victims near Jerusalem. It was with deep emotion that I paused before that tree, silent in my heart for the Holocaust victims, but proud that a great Scandinavian had sacrificed his life in this mission of mercy.

CHAPTER 21

Count Folke Bernadotte – Sweden's Humanitarian Diplomat

SWEDEN HAS HAD MORE THAN ITS SHARE of outstanding people. Up until the nineteenth century, many had been military figures, but during the past two centuries their contributions have largely been humanitarian. Among them, few will rank above Count Folke Bernadotte (1895-1948).

Bernadotte descended from Napoleon's Marshall, Jean Baptiste Jules Bernadotte, who became Sweden's Crown Prince when the Vasa family ran out of male heirs in the early nineteenth century. The Count's great grandfather was a French nobleman who had hoped to become king of France after Napoleon's defeat. Sweden may have been his second choice, but he was a good choice for the Swedes. Taking the name Karl XIV Johan, he was king of both Sweden and Norway from 1818-1844.

Those of us who come from peasant background often have difficulty appreciating the valuable contributions of royal families. We're easily biased by our republican outlook on government. Count Folke Bernadotte is an example of a relative of the royal house of Sweden who took service to his nation and to the world seriously.

As Hitler's "Thousand Year Reich" was crumbling in early 1945, a fearful omen occurred in Norway. Thirty-four patriots were executed in February. This was a sign of Nazi nervousness. Every effort had to be used to get the fifteen Scandinavian prisoners out of the German concentration camps. Living conditions had been vile and the interned Scandinavians were in special danger. Intelligence learned that all prisoners were to be liquidated.

Bernadotte had already proven himself to be a skilled diplomat in Sweden. Now came the biggest challenge he had ever faced. At King Gustav's urging, he arranged a meeting with Heinrich Himmler, head of the feared SS troops, and argued that relations between Sweden and Germany needed improvement. As a token of good will, he presented the Reichsfuehrer with a book on Scandinavian runic inscriptions, a favorite study of the Nazi leader. Bernadotte proposed that the Scandinavian prisoners be allowed to return to their homelands. After some negotiating, Himmler agreed on condition that the Swedes would furnish the transportation. Thus began the famous convoys of white buses with red crosses painted on the roofs and sides. During April 1945, the buses ran continually. Once across the Danish border, they were greeted with food and flowers.

When the war ended, General Eisenhower invited Bernadotte to visit him in Paris. While there he convinced the future president, over Gen. Bedel-Smith's and Gen. Lucius Clay's objections, to allow the Swedish Red Cross to do relief work for German children under age twelve. When the Russians, who were occupying northern Norway, ignored the needs of 100,000 starving Norwegians, Bernadotte went to them with aid. He also supplied ten thousandSoviet soldiers with new uniforms to wear as they were released from German prison camps in Norway. But it was in vain. When they arrived in their homeland, they were mowed down with machine gun fire for having been prisoners. The Communist government did not dare to allow back into their country those who had seen the outside world.

Bernadotte's humanitarian work did not end with the white buses. He helped rescue seventy thousand prisoners who were slaveworkers in the north of Norway. Besides directing the Swedish Red Cross to save Polish and German children, he brought aid to suffering areas of Finland, Hungary, Roumania and Greece. In 1946, he was named Chairman of the Swedish Red Cross. For this service, he never received a salary, only a token stipend. He used his own money for this humanitarian effort.

The great Swedish humanitarian was honored by many governments after the war. Poland awarded him the Order of the White Eagle, reserved for heads of State. No honors, however, came from the Soviet Union, which charged that the Swedish Red Cross was "Pro-Fascist."

In May 1948, Trygve Lie, the United Nations Secretary General, asked Bernadotte to go to Palestine. This was the year that the

British Mandate ended and the State of Israel came into being. This resulted in thousands of Arab refugees. It was a time of bad tempers. Each side was convinced that it was right. Bernadotte, known for his openness to people of all religious creeds, was the right man for the job.

He produced the miracle that brought peace to the land. On June 11, 1948, a cease-fire was accepted by both sides. When asked how this happened, he said: "My father away back home is more than eighty years of age. When I came out here on this job, he gave me a new Bible. And he promised every day to remember me in his prayers. He is not alone. Thousands of Christians have promised to beseech God on my behalf. It is my conviction that without God's help and support this result would never have come about."

On September 17, 1948, 119 days after arriving in the troubled land, he was gunned down by soldiers while passing through Israeli territory at the foot of the "Hill of Evil," where legends say Jesus was tempted. I have been there. Being a "peacemaker" is a high risk profession, but I hope the world will always have such noble minded persons willing to take these risks. Long live the Bernadottes and their kind!

CHAPTER 22

Dag Hammarskjold –
Sweden's 'Apostle Of Peace'

WHAT CAN SMALL NATIONS do for peace in the world? A great deal. That's what we have learned from the life of Sweden's Dag Hammarskjold (1905-1961), pronounced "HA-mer-shold." According to historian T. K. Derry, he "exercised an influence in world affairs as no citizen of a minor European state had yielded before him."

It was a fateful day in September 1961 when the plane carrying Hammerskjold on a peacekeeping mission mysteriously crashed over northern Rhodesia. The world had lost its greatest apostle for peace in our times.

Hammarskjold, son of a Swedish Prime Minister, had a brilliant career from the beginning. A success at college, in teaching and in government service, by age thirty-six he was chairman of the National Bank of Sweden. Outwardly, he had everything going for him.

At age forty-eight, in 1953, he became Secretary General of the United Nations, the most difficult job in the world. He soon distinguished himself by securing the release of United States prisoners in China (from Korea) and by helping to solve the Suez crisis of 1956 between Israel and Egypt. In 1960, he gathered twenty thousand troops from eighteen countries for a successful peacekeeping mission in the Belgian Congo.

What kind of a man was Hammarskjold? Usually, we think that such a person must have been an international "wheeler-dealer," both "compromising" and "compromised." After his death, a book called "Markings" was published. It was his private memoirs of religious reflections. Many people found it hard to believe that Hammarskjold could have had such deep Christian convictions while serving in world politics. The manuscript was found in his New York City apartment together with a letter to a friend giving permission for publication. He called it a "white book concerning my negotiations with myself and with God."

Hammarskjold travelled in the highest circles of the world's power brokers. He would necessarily "compromise," but no one called him a "compromised" person, not even the Soviet Union. They did call him a "murderer" and an "agent of imperialism," but not a "self-seeking" dictator.

The truth is that Hammarskjold was a tender hearted person with strong feelings for the poor and dispossessed, though he had never been either. He felt deeply the criticisms that went with the job. Two convictions motivated his actions: First, that a person has to forget his ego to fulfill life's calling as an instrument of God; and second, that the "way of the Cross," with suffering, sacrifice and humiliation, was the price that he would have to pay. In "Markings," he wrote: "Goodness is something so simple: always to live for others, never to seek one's own advantage." A few months after his death, Dag Hammarskjold was awarded the Nobel Peace Prize.

When we say, "Blessed are the peacemakers," we should remember Dag Hammarskjold. He was one of them. Sweden and Swedes everywhere can be justly proud of this man whose kind is so desperately needed today.

CHAPTER 23

The Myrdals Of Sweden –
Nobel Prize Winners

THE NOBEL PRIZES are among the most coveted recognitions in the world. It's most unusual when a husband and wife each are recognized. This has happened only three times since the prizes were initiated in 1901. Pierre and Marie Curie shared the Nobel Prize for Physics in 1903, and Carl and Gerty Cori shared the 1947 award in medicine. But only once have a husband and wife received separate Nobel prizes.

Gunnar Myrdal (pronounced MEER-dawl) and his wife Alva Reimer Myrdal are the only couple to have received this distinction. Gunnar shared the Nobel Prize for Economics with Friedrich von Hayek in 1974, and Alva shared the 1982 Nobel Peace Prize with Alfonso Garcia Robles.

Mrs. Myrdal (1902-1986) grew up in a middle-class socially conscious family, the daughter of a building contractor and city councilman at Eskilstuna in eastern Sweden. She received her B.A. degree in 1924 and an M.A. in 1934 at the University of Stockholm. Her research was published in a book entitled *The Crisis in the Population Question*. In it she warned about the danger to Sweden because of its dwindling birth rate.

(Karl) Gunnar Myrdal (1898-1987) was born in central Sweden, the son of a railroad employee. He studied law and economics at Stockholm University and so impressed his professors that they named him to the faculty upon graduation. Gunnar and Alva Reimer were married in 1924, the year after he received his law degree. He received a Ph. D. in economics in 1927.

Alva's career began as a schoolteacher, but she is remembered as a sociologist, diplomat and writer. Those who knew her say that she was "engagingly self-confident with an infectious and tinkling laugh." They also said that she had "seemingly unquenchable energy." The book about Sweden's population crisis brought her national attention. She championed the cause of voluntary parenthood and sex education, a daring thing in those days.

In 1955, Mrs. Myrdal was appointed Ambassador to India. There were some who said that it would never work because her social convictions clashed with many conventional Indian views. However, she made a good impression on Prime Minister Jawaharlal Nehru and she received his Award for International Understanding in 1981. Swedish business leaders were impressed with the carefully prepared reports she sent back to Stockholm about trade possibilities.

Alva Myrdal's greatest challenge came in 1961 when the government asked her to become "Special Assistant on Disarmament" to the Swedish Foreign Minister. After being notified of the appointment, she asked that it be kept secret for two weeks while she familiarized herself with the subject. It became her passion for life.

The following year Alva became a member of parliament from the ruling Social Democratic party. She was also named head of the Swedish delegation to the United Nations Disarmament Conference in Geneva. In 1966 she was named to the Swedish Cabinet as minister in charge of disarmament and church affairs. Her book, *The Game of Disarmament: How the United States and Russia Run the Arms Race* (1976), chastised both governments for carrying on an "arms race that has brought costs that are ruinous to the world economy." In addition to the Nobel and Nehru awards, Mrs. Myrdal also received the West German Peace Prize (1970) and the Albert Einstein Peace Prize (1980).

When asked if the long separations from her husband didn't put stress on their marriage, Alva answered that they were deeply interested in each other's work and "we never found anybody else so interesting to talk to." When asked why she continued to be so active in social reform movements for the world, she replied: "If you have a chance to reform things, don't you think you should?"

Mrs. Myrdal kept an interest in youth, even when she was past 80. After receiving the Albert Einstein award she said, "There is a climate of despair that is being forced on the youth of today by the ever-present threat of nuclear war." Concerning this despair, she wrote, "I have never, never allowed myself to give up."

Besides her political work, Alva liked to cook, walk, read poetry and novels, and was attentive to her children. They had a son in Sweden, a daughter in West Germany, and a daughter, Sissella, who is the wife of a former Harvard University president, Derek Bok.

Gunnar had a long and distinguished career as Professor of Economics at the University of Stockholm (1933-1950), General Secretary of the United Nations Economic Commission for Europe (1947-1957), and Director of the Institute for International Economic Studies at the University of Stockholm (1962-1967).

Myrdal was called "the leading economist and social scientist of his epoch" by a *New York Times* writer. He left his influence on America as well as Sweden. One of the charges made against Sweden's high standard of living was that it was responsible for the nation's high suicide rate. Myrdal countered this by saying: "This is a fantastic lie. Why should the protection of your life from economic disasters and from bad health, the opening of education for your people, pensions for the old people, nursery care for children – why should that make you frustrated?"

In 1938 Myrdal accepted an invitation from the Carnegie Corporation to direct a two-year study of Negroes in the United States. He recruited forty-eight writer-scholars for the task. Some of his predictions proved to be wrong. He had been optimistic that Negro rights would be championed by the labor unions and in the North. In the end, he became disillusioned about the American constitution guaranteeing human rights. Still he had great confidence that America would right its wrongs.

Myrdal's major work based on the Carnegie research program was written up in the book, *An American Dilemma: The Negro Problem and Modern Democracy*. The study helped to destroy the "separate but equal" racial policy in the United States. When the Supreme Court gave out its ruling in 1954 that segregation was unconstitutional, the court stated that separate but equal implied enforced inferiority. They cited Myrdal's research as the primary evidence. The work appeared in two large volumes and has been compared with the writings of Toqueville "in its importance as a study of the United States."

Above his desk in Stockholm hung two framed documents: The Declaration of Independence and a citation from Lincoln – "To sin by silence when they should protest makes cowards of men."

He was an early advocate of Keynesian economics which urged governments to improve economic conditions by employing more people. He later abandoned this view since it ignored social justice and was used to support inflationary policies, bringing more problems to the poor.

The Third World's hunger became Myrdal's obsession. He urged that education and social structures were the key to changing this. In his book, *Asian Drama: An Inquiry into the Poverty of the Nations* (1968), he warned that the United States was heading for a disaster in Vietnam. Myrdal claimed that the United States had become a hostage of the Saigon government and urged that America open negotiations with the Communists (which we eventually did anyway). Nonetheless he was a target of Communist derision. They called him "bourgeois," the most derogatory epithet used in *The Communist Manifesto*.

Despite his disappointments with America, he never lost his confidence in it. He stated: "A strong America is a wise America. You are not very good losers. Every time you are losing, an element of insanity enters your thinking that is very dangerous. What you really need is not more private consumption but help for the poor." Interviewed in New York, he said: "America is the one rich country with the biggest slums, the least democratic and least developed health system and the most niggardly attitude against its old people."

I remember Myrdal's comments on America and noted that he was rarely popular with our State Department. We Americans are sensitive about foreigners making judgments about us. However, the issue is this: Was Myrdal correct in his judgments? Agree or disagree about their solutions to social problems, there is no denying that the Myrdals were one of the world's most unusual husband and wife teams.

CHAPTER 24

Swedish-Soviet Relations

SWEDEN AND RUSSIA HAVE KNOWN EACH OTHER for a long time. The Swedish Vikings ventured mainly to the east and onto the rivers of Russia in their quest for trade. They organized the first Russian kingdom at Kiev (modern Ukraine) and gave their own name, "Rus," to the land. Norwegian kings also visited Russia. Both Olaf Tryggvason and Olaf Haraldson (St. Olaf) were in exile among their fellow countrymen in Russia when life was too dangerous back home.

The boundary between Sweden and Russia was often contested. Many battles were fought, the Swedes won a few, but lost more. In 1808, the Russians moved into Finland, then Swedish territory, and occupied it until 1917. With the aid of Kaiser Wilhelm's army, the Finns drove out the Soviets after the Bolshevik revolution.

Sweden remained neutral during both World Wars, but has kept a wary eye on its boundaries to the east. In the last few years, the Soviet navy trespassed Swedish territorial rights many times. This was in spite of the good public relations image that Mikhail Gorbachev had going for him in the West.

Ernest Conine of the *Los Angeles Times* wrote an article entitled "Why are Soviet subs in Swedish waters?" He stated that Soviet "mini-subs have actually landed frogmen on Swedish territory." Soviet defectors, he noted, have said that "in event of a war in Europe, the Soviets would land saboteurs and assassins assigned to eliminate political leaders and key military personnel in enemy countries."

The Swedes took this threat seriously but didn't protest loudly about it. They did, however, move some military personnel into new secret quarters. While the Swedes assured the Soviets that they would not be a part of any aggressive actions against them, they also made it clear that they would fight to defend their territory.

In the late 1970s, the Soviet subs started moving into Swedish territory. A Soviet sub ran aground near the Karlskrona naval base in October 1981. When questioned, the Soviet captain said his radio equipment was broken down and that his gyrocompass and depth gauge were malfunctioning. But six more Soviet subs were discovered in the fjord near Stockholm just a year later. Were they all lost?

What ideas could the Soviet military leaders have had on Swedish territory? Western military experts saw Sweden as a convenient route for an attack on Norway in case of war. Norway is a member of NATO while Sweden is officially neutral. Soviet commandos might have moved in first to attempt to destroy Swedish defenses.

The Swedish policy of neutrality kept them from making an international issue of the Soviet incursions on their territory, even though they were frequently vocal about the foreign policies of other countries. But one has to understand that it is common for small countries to sometimes criticize their friends and be silent towards their potential enemies. The danger is that such silence invites more violations. It's a Scandinavian trait to give subtle signals when they mean to be protesting loudly. A veteran Swedish diplomat, Sverker Astrom, surprised people when he suggested at UCLA that the United States should take the lead in getting the Soviets to stop violating Swedish territory.

To make things look better, Soviet Prime Minister Nikolai Ryzhkov visited Norway and Sweden on a good will tour in January 1988 and settled some old disputes about fishing rights in the Baltic Sea and agreed to supply natural gas to Sweden.

Swedish Prime Minister Ingvar Carlsson issued a warning that "blood will flow" unless the violations stopped. Officially the Soviets denied that any infringements were taking place and that "right wing" elements in Sweden were causing all the trouble. In contrast to Carlsson, the late Prime Minister Olof Palme drew criticism for his neutralism. An article by Henrik Bering-Jensen in the February 8, 1988, issue of "Insight," stated that "Soviet Foreign Minister Andrei Gromyko in Stockholm in January 1984 . . . promised to respect our neutrality policy."

Swedish naval officers complained that they were not allowed to sink the Soviet subs. They were ordered to force the subs to surface instead by dropping the depth charges at a safe distance in order to avoid a diplomatic crisis. Still Soviet submarines kept coming into Swedish waters. Thirty violations were noted in the last half of 1987, some as close as a dozen miles from the business district of Stockholm.

Any visitor to Sweden soon learns that the Swedish people are pro-American even when their government doesn't talk that way. It has been suggested that the Soviets were testing Swedish neutrality to see just how pro-western they were. When Ryzhkov was in Stockholm, he told the Swedes, "Bomb us, by all means." It appears he was taunting them to break their position of neutrality, knowing that the Swedish government would do all in its power to maintain their peace which has lasted for over 170 years.

The Nordic countries were in a difficult position. Denmark and Norway are under the protection of NATO. But their borders are close to the former heavily armed Warsaw Pact nations, whereas the Scandinavians appear to pursue peace like there is no evil to fear.

Finland was the most sensitive of all the Scandinavian countries about its relations to the former Soviet Union. They were careful not to disturb Soviet paranoia. In my visit to Finland and talking to people, they made no hesitations to express their pro-American feelings. I got the impression that they were expecting the United States to be their umbrella against the Soviets even without a formal alliance. The only reason that Finland had any degree of freedom after World War II was because Roosevelt and Churchill denied Stalin's request to include the Finns in the Eastern Block at the Teheran Conference in December 1943. Stalin did admit, according to Charles E. Bohlen's *Witness to History: 1929-1969*, that "any country which fought with such courage for its independence (as Finland) deserved consideration."

All countries operate security and counter-espionage programs against foreign spying activities. The Soviets were experts at espionage and had a strong secret police since the days of the Czars. Peter Wright's book, *Spy Catcher*, claimed that the Soviets penetrated the security systems of most western nations. Wright believes that the head of the British Military Intelligence (MI5) for domestic surveillance was headed for many years by a Soviet agent who was a British citizen. The British government tried to block the publication of Wright's book both in England and Australia.

This information was troubling to us who have family connections in Scandinavia. These are a peace loving people who have often turned "the other cheek." Yet we remember the heroic resistance of Finland and Norway in World War II, and how the Danes frustrated Hitler's attempt to turn them into a "caged canary." During those years, the Swedes assisted their Scandinavian neighbors at considerable cost and risk while maintaining their neutrality. Since the crumbling of the Warsaw Pact and the dismantling of the Soviet Union, most people feel more relaxed about a possible military emergency in the Baltic area. Peace, however, requires courage and it also helps to have some powerful friends.

Swedish/U.S.S.R. parliament buildings.

PART II

*Sweden
And The
Swedish Heritage
In The
'New World'*

CHAPTER 25

John Hanson –
America's First President

ALMOST EVERYONE IN THE WHOLE WORLD knows that George Washington was the first president of the United States. This is one of the first things I learned at school. Why then should this claim be made for someone else? And who was this "John Hanson" anyway? I never read about him in school books. Most books on American history ignore him and he isn't even mentioned in the Encyclopedia Britannica. Did he really exist?

Between Annapolis, Maryland, and the District of Columbia, there is a four lane highway named for John Hanson. The U.S. Postal Service has issued a stamp with his picture. I have some six cent postcards with his picture and inscription "John Hanson – Patriot." So he must have existed.

There are some reasons, however, to ask who John Hanson really was. Historians have been searching the records to clarify his ethnic identity. The consensus that he was an early American of Swedish descent has been challenged and many now think that he was really English. The following story relates the claim as presented by Jacob A. Nelson, a lawyer from Decorah, Iowa, who wrote a book on Hanson in 1939. He admitted that this information was hard to find but claimed that it was verifiable.

Nelson claimed that Hanson was a fourth generation Swedish-American born April 3, 1721, in Maryland. According to Nelson, the Hanson ancestry can be traced to Yorkshire, England, in the middle of the thirteenth century. That was where the Danes had their kingdom (Danelaw) a few centuries earlier. The name was changed to Hanson, meaning "son of Henry," about 1340. The Hansons moved to Sweden and intermarried with the royal family. A Colonel John Hanson was killed in the battle of Lutzen, November 16, 1632, defending King Gustavus Adolphus. The king also died that same day. In 1642, Queen Christina sent four of Hanson's sons to Maryland to join the Swedish settlers on the banks of the Delaware River. The colony, known as "New Sweden," had been founded in 1638. Later on the Dutch and then the English took control of Maryland. In her book, *Finns in North America*, Eloise Engle notes that a part of Hanson's ancestry goes back to Swedes who lived in Finland. At that time, Finland was governed by Sweden.

The Hansons were highly ambitious and capable colonists. They were active in government and were successful farmers. Samuel Hanson, John's father, was a member of the Maryland General Assembly, a sheriff and held other offices.

The Hanson home had an air of aristocracy about it. Yet they were well liked by their neighbors for their honesty and patriotism. Patriotism, of course, meant loyalty to King George of England. They were also known for their piety. Every day they gathered for Bible reading and prayer. By the time John was twelve, he had memorized long sections of the Bible, the catechism and many hymns. There is a tradition that young John was educated at Oxford University in England.

After marriage and settling down with his family, John became active in Maryland politics. Though loyal to British rule, he sided with the colonists in the grievances against the mother country. He was strongly opposed to the "Stamp Act Congress" that met in New York. Among his close acquaintances were Ben Franklin, Thomas Jefferson, the Adams' and other early colonial leaders. After the British reprisals against the people of Boston for the "Tea Party," Hanson sent a substantial gift of silver for the relief of the people.

Hanson was a leader in the independence movement of the colonies. When the Continental Congress was formed, he became the first president. On a memorial plaque at the Frederick County Courthouse in Maryland, he is remembered as "President of the United States in Congress Assembled, November 5, 1781 to November 4, 1782," and as a signer of the Articles of Confederation.

George Washington sent President Hanson a letter of congratulations and promised him his loyalty in leading the new government. He signed the letter: "Your most obedient servant, George

Washington." Hanson's confidence in Washington was also unqualified. He wrote: "We will win the war with George Washington in the field, if we do our share at home. In the end we will establish an Inseparable Union, and ultimately it will become the greatest nation in the world." Two of his sons gave their lives for the cause of this freedom.

If you visit Washington, D.C., you can find John Hanson's statue in the Capitol building. Pause a moment before it and remember this early American patriot who gave so much for his country. And who knows, maybe some hard evidence will turn up in some long lost archives that will once and for all settle the argument about his ethnic identity. In the meantime, many Scandinavians are unmoved in the belief that he was one of them.

SWEDEN AND THE SWEDISH HERITAGE IN THE 'NEW WORLD'

CHAPTER 26

Scandinavian Immigrants
And The Slavery Issue

I HAD ALWAYS WONDERED why the Scandinavians settled mainly north of the Mason-Dixon line. A review of the editorial opinions expressed in the Scandinavian newspapers from the 1840s to 1870s reveals a great deal about the attitudes of those immigrants. The Scandinavians were very outspoken on the slavery issue. One of the most influential early writers was Ole Rynning. His *True Account of America*, published in 1838, sparked an outbreak of "America Fever" in Scandinavia. He predicted that there would be "either a separation between the northern and southern states or bloody civil disputes."

The nineteenth century saw a great clamor for the freedoms of the common person in the Scandinavian countries and the immigrants were outspoken in their denunciation of slavery. They claimed that Negroes "are redeemed by the same blood and are destined to inherit the same glory as other races." Three Wisconsin counties, Racine, Walworth and Waukesha, voted to approve Negro suffrage in 1847. This was an area where the Scandinavians predominated. The state, however, turned down the referendum, for fear that Wisconsin would become a haven for runaway slaves.

The slavery issue was the main reason why most Scandinavians settled in the northern states, according to Arlow William Andersen, author of *The Immigrant Takes His Stand*. Anderson was a professor at Jamestown College in North Dakota.

Until the mid 1850s, Scandinavians tended to vote with the Democratic party. However, as the tension over slavery heightened, most of them became Republicans and were solid supporters of Abraham Lincoln. They were equally pro-Union and anti-slavery. Only a few settled in the South and some of them did own slaves, but not many.

The Scandinavians never got on the bandwagon with Horace Greeley and the other radical abolitionists. They were also suspicious of America's expansionist foreign policy. They did not support the war with Mexico since they suspected it was a subterfuge to expand the number of slave states. Most Scandinavians expected slavery to die a natural death since it was becoming economically unprofitable. While the number of Scandinavians was not great at the outbreak of the Civil War, they rallied to the cause of the Union with fierce loyalty. The Fifteenth Wisconsin Regiment, made up of over 800 Scandinavians, commanded by Col. Hans Heg from Racine County, distinguished themselves in gallantry. Heg was killed at the Battle of Chickamauga (Georgia) in 1863.

Defenders of slavery claimed constitutional authority and justified it on humanitarian and religious grounds. They pointed to the Ten Commandments which spoke of menservants and maidservants, and to the lack of any prohibition of slavery in the Bible. Some of them claimed that slavery to Christian masters was a blessing, since many of the Africans had converted to the Christian faith. The Scandinavian editors of the North did not accept these claims.

The most tragic arguments were in the churches. The Baptist, Methodist, and Presbyterian churches divided over the slavery question. A crisis developed among the Norwegian Synod Lutherans whose theological students attended Concordia Seminary in St. Louis. The students returned to the North indoctrinated in pro-slavery views. They didn't actually claim so much that slavery was "right," but rather that it was "not wrong," according to the Bible. They also supported the sovereign rights of states and the Dred Scott decision of the Supreme Court in 1857.

When these students returned North, they were challenged by the congregations, and especially by the editors of secular Scandinavian newspapers. There were some heated debates at the Synod conventions in Wisconsin and Iowa in those days. When the Union Army closed Concordia Seminary (1861) for its pro-slavery views, the Norwegian Synod established Luther College in Decorah, Iowa. In 1876, steps were taken to build its own seminary.

Eighty years after the war between the states, I encountered this same pro-slavery position with a college teacher whose tradition had been in the Norwegian Synod. A hundred years after the war, while enrolled for graduate studies at Concordia Seminary, all traces of pro-slavery views were gone. I was surprised, however, that students commented so openly on the pro-slavery views of Dr. C. F. W. Walther, whom I had held in high esteem.

Tuve Nilsson Hasselquist, a Lutheran pastor and a journalist, had great influence in bringing Swedish immigrants into the Republican party over the slavery issue. The Swedes, like their Scandinavian neighbors, found slavery an intolerable social system. Claus Clausen, a Danish schoolteacher who became a pastor in the Norwegian Synod, served as a chaplain with the Fifteenth Wisconsin Regiment. He was an anti-slavery leader in the Synod until his resignation in 1868 when the Synod pastors still refused to take a stand against the principle of slavery. Clausen was pastor in my grandmother's congregation near Blooming Prairie, Minnesota, after the war.

Now I understand a little better why I was destined to be born in North Dakota and to become acclimatized to its long winters, rather than to the balmy climate of the South where the magnolias and dogwoods grace the skyline.

CHAPTER 27

Abraham Lincoln And The Scandinavian Immigrants

THE EARLY SCANDINAVIAN IMMIGRANTS were uncommitted to any of the American political parties and distrusted the new nation's foreign policies. But as Abraham Lincoln moved to the fore among the politicians, they rallied to his support and never wavered. Even when many of the newspapers attacked the president's leadership, the Scandinavians remained loyal to him. Carl Fredrik Solberg, editor of *Emigranten* (*The Emigrant*), hailed Lincoln as "one of the greatest men of our century."

The election of 1860 saw the Democrats hopelessly split. Lincoln was not the best known presidential aspirant of the new Republican Party, but he had fewer enemies. His "house divided" speech about the nation and slavery, won the support of the freedom loving immigrants. Scandinavians opposed the Fugitive Slave Law which required runaway slaves to be returned to their owners. Other concerns of the Scandinavians were the homestead act and a moderate protective tariff. This benefitted the North and the West.

There was talk of annexing Cuba in those days. This was opposed by Solberg because it appeared to be a ruse to extend slavery, as the island would be admitted as a slave state. The "Know-Nothing" movement was directed against immigrants and wanted to delay their receiving citizenship and the right to vote. Lincoln opposed this movement. Upon Lincoln's election, Solberg wrote: "A thousand hurrahs for Lincoln and Hamlin!" Hamlin was vice president during Lincoln's first term. Solberg wrote in glowing terms of Lincoln's inaugural address that it was "as good as 10,000 men."

When the Confederate forces attacked Ft. Sumpter in the Charleston harbor on April 12, 1861, Solberg wrote, "To arms!" He declared, "Fear not that the cause is not righteous and good. God is on the side of the American soldier." While the number of

Scandinavians was relatively small at the time of the Civil War, their participation was high. On the basis of percentage, they had more people in the Union Army than the "Yankees."

The leadership of Col. Hans Heg encouraged the Scandinavians in Wisconsin to rally for Lincoln's cause. It was Heg's opinion that the men who conducted the war would be the ones to control postwar affairs. He argued that Scandinavians must get into the fight if they hoped to occupy influential positions later. He wrote in a newspaper, "Let us unite in giving to posterity untarnished the old honorable name of Norsemen." In the field balloting of the 15th Wisconsin Regiment under Heg's command, the Scandinavians voted overwhelmingly in the Republican column to support Lincoln.

When Lincoln issued his Emancipation Proclamation to take effect on New Year's Day 1863, the full document was published in the *Emigranten*. The newspaper described Lincoln as "a Christian and a patriotic man." When the election of 1864 came, the Scandinavians were fully committed to the support of the President against General McClellan, the Democratic candidate. McClellan had pledged peace between the two divisions of the nation, while Lincoln held out for victory to save the Union.

Knud J. Fleischer, editor of *Faedrelandet* (*The Fatherland*), wrote that if anyone voted for McClellan, people would point to his gravestone and say, "There lies one of those who, blind and confused in party strife, voted for McClellan and immediate peace, thereby fostering eternal war." After Lincoln's death, Fleischer laid the blame on the Democratic party. He cited a 1864 Democratic campaign statement which read: "If he in the future as in the past misgoverns the nation, he never will live to complete his term." It seemed all too prophetic for the Scandinavian press. Solberg laid the blame on the Confederates. The Scandinavian press reflected the loyalty to Lincoln that characterized the majority of its constituency.

No Scandinavian has done more to immortalize Lincoln than Carl Sandburg (1878-1967). Born of Swedish parents in Galesburg, Illinois, he wrote six large volumes on Lincoln's *Prairie Years* (1926) and the *War Years* (1939). He was awarded the Pullitzer prize for history in 1940 for the "War Years." While Sandburg was born thirteen years after Lincoln's death, he said he came to learn first hand as a boy about Lincoln's times from veterans who fought under Grant and Sherman.

Sandburg was a newspaper man and became an editorial writer with the *Chicago Daily News,* founded by a Norwegian, Victor F. Lawson. His fascination with Lincoln was possibly because they were both from Illinois. However, I believe that he was also reflecting the general Scandinavian regard for Lincoln as one of the world's greatest heroes. He did solid research on Lincoln history, studying the more than one million words written by the President, more than in the Bible with the Apocrypha. President Franklin D. Roosevelt personally conducted Sandberg to the Lincoln corners of special interest in the White House in 1937. President Herbert Hoover did the same in 1930. There seems hardly a thing about Lincoln that Sandburg didn't uncover.

I don't know how many Scandinavian immigrants Mr. Lincoln might have known, but they certainly held him in high esteem as the "savior" of the Republic.

"The Great Emancipator." 87

CHAPTER 28

John Ericsson And The Civil War's Great Naval Battle

THE BATTLE OF HAMPTON ROADS in Virginia is remembered as one of the most important naval encounters in history. It cannot, however, be compared to the great battles of Jutland, Midway or the Coral Sea in the number of warships and personnel. But its significance made every navy in the world obsolete. It was fought by just two strange looking and dissimilar warships between the Confederate's "Merrimac" and the Union's "Monitor." The battle lasted about four hours and the casualties were only a few wounded.

What was the Civil War naval battle all about and why is it remembered? What has it got to do with the Scandinavian heritage?

President Lincoln was pale and visibly shook. Panic was overtaking some of the cabinet members, including Edwin Stanton, Secretary of War. Bad news had come to Washington. For months it had been rumored that the Confederacy was building a fearful new weapon – an ironclad warship!

It was March 8, 1862. Two Union warships, the "Cumberland" and the "Congress," sailed out to stop this dreadful sea monster. Their cannonballs bounced harmlessly off its slanted iron covered sides which protected its ten cannons. In short order, both Union warships were sunk with much loss of life. President Lincoln's strategy for defeating the South through a naval blockade hung in the balance. If this plan failed, the war could drag on for many years or it might even mean the end of the "United States of America." Secretary Stanton gave a doomsday speech to the President and his colleagues. Every ship and seaport city of the North, he claimed, were in imminent danger of destruction. Both Lincoln and Stanton paced the floor, looking out the window to the Potomac River, as though the dreaded warship were soon to arrive.

One cabinet member, Gideon Welles, appeared unruffled by the news. As the Secretary of the Navy, he had a secret. Naval intelligence was well aware of what the "rebs" were doing. Now it was the Navy Secretary's turn to speak. He advised calm since the Confederate warship's size was too deep to sail up the Potomac and it was not seaworthy enough to reach New York. Then he told them that the Union was also building an "ironclad." One of the cabinet members asked: "How many guns does it have?" "Two," replied Welles. Horrified unbelief came over Stanton.

The next day, large crowds gathered to watch the "Merrimac" (renamed the "Virginia") return for battle against the Union fleet at the mouth of the James River at Hampton Roads, Virginia. It headed directly to finish off the badly damaged S.S. Minnesota. Out of nowhere a strange looking craft appeared. Some called it a "Yankee cheese box on a raft." The U.S.S. Monitor's two cannons took about seven minutes to prepare for firing each cannonball. Five times the Merrimac rammed the smaller vessel. Its iron frame held. Volleys were exchanged with some damage to both ships. At noon, the Monitor withdrew from battle and the Merrimac was almost out of cannonballs, so it left the Minnesota and sailed off claiming victory. But the North interpreted the news differently. The little Monitor had done its job. The mighty Merrimac had been stopped! Lincoln was ecstatic and the North was jubilant.

The architect of that strange looking and quickly constructed Union craft was John Ericsson. He had been born in Varmland, Sweden, July 13, 1803. Though of errascible temperament, he became famous for his inventive skills by the time he was thirteen. At age twenty-three he was honored in London. At thirty-six, he emigrated to America. Among his two thousand inventions was an improved model of the screw propeller which was to power large ships. He died in 1889.

What effect could such a little duel have on history? It marked the beginning of a new age in ship building. In London, the battle was talked about by everyone. As a result, the British built a new ironclad navy. They had experimented with a few models, but the Monitor/Merrimac clash was the clincher. This was also one of the first naval battles fought by two steam powered ships, also one of Ericsson's projects.

It was, I suppose, only proper that a Scandinavian inventor should have made such a contribution to the future navies of the world. Afterall, they had built the "longships."

How did Secretary Welles discover this "classic genius inventor," as historian Page Smith described him? Would you believe that it was a Harvard professor of pastoral theology named Horace Bushnell who made the introduction? He and Welles had been long time friends.

Don't underestimate the value of old friends. They can turn out to be your greatest asset. Just remember the panic in the president's cabinet and the Swedish inventor who saved the day. And if you visit Stockholm, see for yourself the proud statue the Swedes have erected of Ericsson by the harbor.

CHAPTER 29

A Swedish Immigrant
Writes Home

DIARIES AND LETTERS HAVE BECOME a valuable source of information for writing histories. Richard K. Hofstrand has published a fictionalized biography of his grandfather, Martin Hofstrand, who settled near Brinsmade in Benson County of North Dakota in 1883, entitled *With Affection, Marten*. It is written in the form of immigrant letters sent to relatives in Sweden. He states that the "people, places, times and events" are real.

The story begins in Malmohus County in southern Sweden, across from Copenhagen. Times were hard in 1882. Work was almost impossible for a young man to find. He wrote: "Too much of the land belongs to the nobility. They own most of it! And because they don't have to pay any taxes, they keep more of the money than poor peasants such as we." This describes the cause of much Swedish immigration.

"America Fever" was fanned by railway agents sent to recruit immigrants. They painted rosey pictures of free land and prosperity for everyone. Immigrants took a large trunk with clothes, food and some tools. They also needed fifty dollars of American money to clear customs.

When Martin arrived in America with two brothers in June 1883, his first big decision was what name to take. He said "Hovstrand," but the immigration officer wrote "Hofstrand."

The early days on the one 160-acre homestead were no paradise. It was hard work and a ten by six foot tar paper shack was no prairie Hilton. It cost $200 to file a land claim. A well had to be dug and a year of residence was required before ownership became final. Good crops and prices did not happen every year. In January 1885, one of North Dakota's famous three day blizzards hit. There was nothing for Martin to do but wait inside until it was over. To leave the shack was suicide. Such cold weather as minus thirty degrees was unknown in southern Sweden.

It took five years for Martin to persuade his sweetheart to cross the Atlantic, supposedly to visit her sister in the same community. It took additional convincing to get her to agree to join his life on the prairie.

The Hofstrands had to make a major decision. Would they be "Swedish" or "American" in the New World? They chose to speak English but never lost their love for the Swedish heritage. The annual Swedish picnic was often held at the Hofstrand farm. Like many Scandinavians, they were great believers in education.

The "letters" from America were often weekly in the beginning. But when family and farming operations took more time, correspondence declined to an annual Christmas letter.

There were tears on the prairie too. One of the boys, age twelve, stepped on a rusty nail and died from lockjaw. (I remember how my father used to warn me about such dangers.) The story traces the change from oxen and horses to tractors, from kerosene lamps to the thirty-two volt Delco plant, and from the buggy to the Model T Ford. The pictures of pioneer days in the book add a great deal of delight. The author has given us an interesting and realistic picture of what it was like when grandpa and grandma began life on the prairies.

CHAPTER 30

Impressions Of 'Native Americans' By Swedish Immigrants

I GREW UP ON A FARM ten miles west of Ft. Abercrombie, in southeastern North Dakota. During the days of the New Deal's Public Works Administration, the fort was restored and there was a big seventy-fifth celebration in 1937 to remember the "massacre" of 1862. It was quite a party. Prof. Edward Milligan, Superintendent of Schools in nearby Colfax, led the Indian dances.

By the time I was growing up, our contacts with Native Americans was on a very civil basis. I remember that my father had a hired man one year whose mother was a Sioux. He looked every bit a "Native American" and was accepted as one of our family.

Things were not that simple, however, when the first immigrants arrived. Sweden sent more of its people to America than any other Scandinavian country, 1,200,000. Some of the Swedish impressions with the Indians are preserved in letters collected from the immigrant period (1840-1914).

Life in the New World was quite a shock to the highly civilized Swedes. American shysters and swindlers of every sort were set to pounce on unwary immigrants. They had already victimized many of the Native Americans and this caused the immigrants to be in double jeopardy as they travelled across the prairie trails. They also witnessed the savage reprisals against the Indians and the "trail of broken treaties."

Prof. H. Arnold Barton of Southern Illinois University has written that "though they sometimes feared the red man, there is little evidence that they hated or despised him. On the whole relations were peaceable and the Swedes tended both to respect the Indian and to sympathize with his lot."

One young man, Carl Friman, wrote home to Sweden from Salem, Wisconsin, that the immigrants and the Indians used to hunt deer together. Another immigrant, Peter Cassel, wrote home that the government had purchased land from Indians south of Mt. Pleasant, Iowa, where they intended to establish a Swedish colony. They did and I have driven through this well kept community many times while travelling to St. Louis.

Those about to emigrate from both Sweden and Norway were warned, especially by the clergy, that their trip would be full of dangers. If they did not fall into the hands of Turkish pirates or suffer shipwreck on the way over, the impenetrable forests of America would offer "ferocious wild beasts and bloodthirsty Indians" as their only neighbors.

Other pastors, however, left the security of the state church in Sweden and endured the frontier life. Sometimes they travelled for many days and over many miles of trackless territory to minister to scattered groups of immigrants. One of their anxieties in leaving home was the Indians who sometimes silently entered their houses wanting food. The pastor's wife and children learned how to appear brave. More often than not, all they wanted was food and tobacco, with no intent to do harm.

But people travelling the 1,800 miles from Iowa to California for gold encountered thousands of warriors looking for the scalps of lonely travellers. A poisoned arrow found many a mark and harnesses were cut away to steal horses. In 1867, August Andren led a group of Scandinavians into western Nebraska to make railroad ties. At the first suspicious noise around the campfire at night, the order was given to put out the fire as well as their pipes. When no squaws or papooses were with the travelling Indians, the immigrants soon learned to beware. That may be a war party! That same summer, the Indians pulled up the tracks and attacked a train when it derailed. Peter Nyman, writing home from Duluth, Minnesota, told how he was released by his Indian captors after turning over the supply of chewing tobacco he had bought in town for the men in the logging camp. This did not make him a hero back in the camp.

George F. Erickson wrote back to Sweden in 1910 about a story he'd heard in America. A Yankee was boasting to a Swede about the greatness of America. No matter what he claimed, the Swede said, "We have exactly the same thing in Sweden." Finally, the American became angry and said, "I know one thing you don't have in Sweden, you don't have any Indians!" Not to be outdone, the Swede replied, "We have Indians in Sweden, too, but we call them Norwegians."

CHAPTER 31

The Swedes Of
Jamestown, New York

MY FRIEND, PAUL SETTERGREN, stopped by for a visit before he moved to Jamestown, New York. He brought a book for me to read, entitled *Saga From the Hills: A History of the Swedes of Jamestown*. Its seven hundred pages offer insight on all Swedes who came to America.

Sweden was generous to the New World. One million two hundred thousand Swedes (twenty-five percent of the population) came to America. The earliest Swedish communities began on the Delaware river in the 1638. They were not, however, allowed to live in peace. The Dutch and then the English grabbed their territory and they did not continue to expand as a Swedish colony.

Two hundred years later, starting in the 1840s, when the large movement of immigrants were arriving, the Swedes were determined to remember their culture and heritage. They started coming to Jamestown in 1850. Wilton E. Bergstrand offered five reasons for this choice: 1) The natural beauty; 2) healthful climate; 3) fresh water; 4) valuable forests; 5) and good farmland.

But why did they leave their homeland? First, the upper classes (nobility, gentry and government officials) had most of the privileges. In America, they could vote. Second, military duty was required for men at age nineteen and Sweden had been involved in many continental wars. They weren't cowards, but like Scandinavians since time immemorial, they didn't like being ordered by authorities what they didn't have personal convictions to do. More than three thousand immigrants from Sweden fought to free the slaves in America's Civil War. Third, they wanted to get away from the state church system. Though there were many faithful and effective clergy, the men of the cloth were seen as a class aligned with the nobility and as opposed to social change. While the immigrants loved their native land, America meant a new start for them in a world of freedom and opportunity.

The Swedes were welcome in Jamestown because they brought needed skills in wood and metal working. Soon they became executives and owners of businesses. They also had a reputation for great physical strength. One Swedish immigrant bought a stove, had it strapped on his back and carried the 250 pound load to his house on top of Swede Hill.

I asked Settergren (himself a Swede) how many Swedish people live in the Jamestown area. He estimated about 35,000. That rivals Rockford, Illinois, another strong Swedish-American community.

The Swedes were considered desirable settlers because they had a reputation for honesty. They were noted for being hard workers and having respect for the law. They were strong community builders. They were also an inventive people. One of the Jamestown settlers, Karl Peterson, invented the Crescent line of tools.

Christian faith was important to Swedish immigrants. They built over two thousand churches in America, the largest being First Lutheran in Jamestown. One Swedish farmer near Jamestown came to pay his bill at the store after harvest and was asked by the storekeeper if he wanted a receipt. "No, God knows I have paid my bill," he replied. The storekeeper sneered, "Do you still believe in God?" Confessing to be a believer, he asked: "Don't you?" When the storekeeper replied "Naw!" the farmer said, "Then you better give me a receipt." He wasn't taking chances.

Early Swedish-American settlements.

CHAPTER 32

The American
Swedish Institute

ONE OF THE PROUD PLACES in Minneapolis is the American Swedish Institute at 2600 Park Avenue. It was founded in 1929 by Swan J. Turnblad "to promote and preserve the Swedish heritage in America." It has about seven thousand members. They have an excellent publication called the *ASI Posten* which appears ten times a year. The Institute is headquartered in one of the most elegant buildings in the Middle West.

Even if you don't live in Minnesota, you might want to get acquainted with this organization if you are of Swedish background or if you are interested in Scandinavian culture. However, if you live in the Twin Cities, there are many direct benefits: Free admission to the museum, invitations to special events and exhibits, discounts on gift purchases, language study and travel discounts, besides a subscription to the newsletter.

One of the special features to the *Posten* is the column entitled, "Sag Det Pa Svenska!" ("Say it in Swedish!") Did you know that "en forening" means "an organization" or "association?" Or that "en ordforande" means "a chairman?" Or that "en dragspelare" was "an accordion player?" By studying these columns each month, a person can gain a good working knowledge of Swedish in a couple of year's membership.

The Institute offers scholarships for young people who attend the Swedish Camp called "Sjolunden." It's a part of Concordia College's International Language Villages. Besides the two-week and the four-week language study programs in Minnesota, they also offer a month of traveling in Sweden.

The Institute offers classes in the Swedish language, folk art, folk fiddling and Swedish exercises. In 1985, which was the year of Bach, a special nine week class on the famous composer was held. Travel to Sweden is an important part of their ethnic heritage. The Institute promotes such tours with special rates to members.

101

As would be expected, the Swedish Lucia Festival (December 13) is a gala event in the Institute's social program. Beautiful Swedish young women dress up in their prettiest to compete for the crown. Tickets to this event are limited and every year has a sellout.

The Institute is a member of the Swedish Council of America which sponsors a "Swedish Week" and publishes a quarterly journal entitled *Sweden & America*. In 1984, the "Swedish Week" was celebrated in Seattle, and His Royal Highness Prince Bertil of Sweden was awarded America's "Swede of the Year." The "Great Swedish Heritage Award" was presented to actress Ann Margret and Nobel Laureate Glenn T. Seaborg.

The Swedes are rightfully proud of Raoul Wallenberg for his heroic effort to save more than 100,000 Hungarian Jews from Nazi death camps. The Institute featured an exhibit of his work in 1985. If you are going to Minneapolis, it will be worth your time to visit this fine center of Swedish culture.

I'm proud to be a member of the American Swedish Institute, even though my ethnic heritage is Norwegian. I have great admiration for Sweden and the Swedish heritage. So I am grateful that ASI welcomes the many friends of Sweden and Swedish culture into their ranks. But then, I'm prejudiced. We have a charming daughter-in-law and three handsome grandsons who claim the Swedish heritage.

CHAPTER 33

The 'Independent Order Of Vikings'

SCANDINAVIANS HAVE BEEN COMING TO AMERICA since the days of Leif Erikson. But up until the war between the states, most of them melted into the English speaking world. After the war, when they came in large numbers and formed strong ethnic communities, they began to organize into fraternal groups to preserve their Old World values.

Eleven immigrants of Swedish descent organized the "Independent Order of Vikings" in Chicago on June 2, 1890. They had as their goals: "Unity of fellowship, help in time of need, and a sound investment in the future." Though founded by Swedes, who still make up the largest part of the membership, since 1951 all Scandinavians and spouses have been welcomed into its fellowship. In the latter part of the nineteenth century, the "Windy City" became a Mecca especially for Danes, Norwegians and Swedes who came to seek their fortunes in the New World.

These early immigrants were mostly young and adventurous folk who had advanced social ideas. One of their first projects was to organize a fraternal society called "Vikingarne" to pay sick benefits and funeral assistance to immigrants. Then they set up a "reading club" for the intellectual advancement of their people so they could get ahead in an English speaking society. In more recent times they have established scholarships for high school students whose families are members. They also give a full tuition grant for a member to attend the International Summer School at the prestigious Uppsala University in Sweden.

Fiercely proud of their Scandinavian roots, these "Vikings" erected a statue of a prominent Swede, Carl von Linne, which stands in Chicago's Lincoln Park along Lake Michigan. In 1892, the name of the organization was changed to the "Independent Order of Vikings" in order to identify with the culture of their new land.

It wasn't long before new lodges sprung up in the Chicago area where six are active today. Fifty-two local lodges make up the organization in 16 states including Colorado, Connecticut, Illinois, Indiana, Iowa, Massachusetts, Michigan, Missouri, Nebraska, New Hampshire, New Jersey, New York, Oregon, Utah, Washington and Wisconsin. Many of the lodges own the buildings where they meet. A newsletter called the *Viking Journal* is published monthly.

The heart of the organization is a life insurance program. This springs from the immigrant days when the Scandinavians needed to look out for each other in a strange world. Junior Clubs for young people under age sixteen sponsor sporting events, dinners, parties and instruction sessions to learn Scandinavian dances.

As you would expect, the Independent Order of Vikings is famous for its smorgasbords. Any Scandinavian holiday is an excuse to bring out the food, but especially Christmas, Lucia Day (December 13), Midsummer Day (June 26) and the Oktoberfest.

Every two years a national convention is held. Seventeen officers and members of the Executive Council are elected to govern and promote the organization. I'm indebted to Kristen Johnson of Quincy, Massachusetts, for information on this organization. If you wish to know more about this proud group of Scandinavians, write to their headquarters: Independent Order of Vikings, 200 East Ontario Street, Room 207, Chicago, Illinois 60611. They're people worth knowing.

Independent Order of Vikings logo.

CHAPTER 34

Charles Lindbergh And
The 'Spirit Of St. Louis'

"THE LAST HERO," is the way biographer Walter S. Ross described Charles Augustus Lindbergh. There is no doubt about the hero status of this tall, handsome and boyish-looking Swede from Minnesota. When Lindbergh returned to New York after his triumphant flight to Paris, he was greeted with the city's greatest parade. It's estimated that up to 4,500,000 admirers lined the sidewalks leading to Central Park on June 13, 1927, and more than 3,500,000 pounds of ticker tape was dropped on his entourage. The first air mail stamp was dedicated to him. Honors were given him by the governments of the United States, France, and Germany, as well as private recognitions.

That was a turbulent time and America needed a hero. Historian Page Smith, now retired from UCLA, has written "the times had been difficult and demoralizing ones," noting that "many thoughtful Americans despaired of the future of the Republic." He stated that "leaders were in disrepute, politicians, alive and dead, had come under severely critical scrutiny." The young flier from Little Falls had captured the world and taken people's minds off their troubles.

In his autobiography, *We*, Lindbergh wrote about his family background. Their name in Sweden had been Manson. Grandpa Ola Manson, born in 1810, was a peasant farmer who broke loose from his economic servitude and was elected to the Riksdag (parliament) at age 39. He struck up a friendship with the Crown Prince, who became King Charles XV in 1859, and was named his secretary. A man of high principles, his goal in government was to campaign for social reform. He succeeded in outlawing the whipping posts. He fought to make it illegal for employers to beat their hired help and tried to get voting privileges for people other than the nobility, clergy, farmers and property owners.

The privileged classes were enraged at his efforts and managed to trump up charges of embezzlement against him where he was a loan officer in a bank at Malmo (across from Copenhagen).

When he'd had enough of the reactionary spirit prevailing in his homeland, Manson, now Lindbergh, took his family to Sauk Centre, Minnesota, in 1860, where he built a twelve- by sixteen-foot log cabin. This was quite a comedown in lifestyle. Before leaving Sweden, members of the parliament gave him a medal made of solid gold. After arriving in America, he traded the medal for a plow. Trinkets meant nothing to him.

Those sterling qualities were passed on to his children. His son, Charles August Lindbergh, Sr., named after the king of Sweden, became a lawyer and made his home in Little Falls. Later he was elected to the United States Congress five times, defeated only because he voted to oppose America's entry into World War I. His wife had degrees from the Michigan and Columbia Universities. She had gone to Little Falls to teach chemistry. Her father was the pioneer of porcelain dental art and had a successful dental practice in Detroit.

Charles, Jr., was born February 4, 1902, in Detroit. Because of his father's political career, he never attended a full year of school in one place until he entered the University of Wisconsin. After a year and a half, young Charles decided that the University was no place for him. His interests were his motorcycle, gun, open fields and especially the sky. So he enrolled in a flying school in Lincoln, Nebraska, against the wishes of his father; but his mother thought it was great and went barnstorming with him around the country. At the Army Air school at Brooks Field, Texas, Charles graduated at the head of his class in 1925.

Six years earlier, a New York financier had offered a prize of $25,000 for the first successful air flight from New York to Paris. Charles was determined to win it. Some young St. Louis financiers backed his effort and they ordered a plane with a two hundredhorsepower radial air-cooled engine with navigating instruments to be built in San Diego. The plane was named "The Spirit of St. Louis" to show his appreciation for their backing. Bernt Balchen, the famous Norwegian aviator, helped him with the flight plan.

En route to New York, he landed at Lambert Field in St. Louis. A replica of the plane is on display at the Lambert Field Terminal in St. Louis, as well as at The Minneapolis International Airport. The original plane is in the Smithsonian Institute in Washington, D.C. The plane's top speed was 130 miles per hour and its four hundred gallons of gasoline had a range of about 4,000 miles. Paris was 3,500 miles away. He took off from Roosevelt Airfield on Long Island at 7:54 a.m. on May 20, 1927, and landed at Le Bourget in Paris after a flight of 33 and a half hours.

That was a daring adventure by any standards. It had never been done before and his chief competitors for the prize were planning to fly trimotor planes with extra crew. In his autobiography, Lindbergh wrote that his greatest challenge was sleep. He went to a hotel in New York to get some rest before the flight, but a friend came to visit him. Landing in Paris, however, proved to be even more dangerous. The huge crowds had to be held back by the police or they would have torn him apart, they were in such a celebrating mood. He was rescued and driven to the American Embassy, but someone stole his log book out of the plane. It was never recovered.

Lindbergh became an instant hero. Then came the dark days. I remember being told by our rural grade schoolteacher that Lindberg had gone to Europe and was invited to inspect the air forces of England, Russia, France and Germany. Unfortunately, he wasn't a sophisticated diplomat. He didn't say what the western press wanted to hear. Lindbergh praised Germany's Luftwaffe as the best air force in the world. The Nazis were delighted and decorated him for it. Immediately, he was branded pro-Hitler and anti-democratic. I can also remember Dorothy Thompson, a popular newscaster during World War II, saying, "I am absolutely certain that Lindbergh hates the present democratic system."

Nothing could have been further from the truth and history soon vindicated Lindbergh's judgment. If Billy Mitchell hadn't worked furiously to build up Britain's Royal Air Force, Hitler would have had his way during the London blitz of 1940. The American press, unfortunately, had always suspected Scandinavians of being pro-German, and especially the Swedes, as many Germans still live in Stockholm. Norwegians were likewise so accused during World War I. Scandinavians have a reputation for independent thinking and feel no debts to this day to agree even with their allies on all points. Lindbergh campaigned hard to keep the United States out of the war. His strong anti-Soviet views seem to have been a part of his "America First" rally participation in Madison Square Garden in May 1941. From our present perspective, we'd have to say that Lindbergh was politically "unwise." Still he was no friend of the Nazis. For his convictions, he was denied a United States Air Force commission during World War II.

Famous people are often targets of tragedy. Charles and his devoted wife, Anne Morrow Lindbergh, had their greatest heartbreak when their son, Charles, Jr., was kidnapped on March 1, 1930, just twenty months old. The story of the German carpenter from New York, Bruno Richard Hauptmann, in whose home was found $13,000 of the $50,000 ransom money, was front page news for years. People's hearts went out to the Lindberghs so much that even the noted Chicago gangster, Al Capone and his wife, offered $10,000 to get the child back. The body was found on May 16, 1932. Hauptmann was arrested in September 1934 and convicted. I can't remember anyone mourning his death in the electric chair on April 3, 1936. The media, however, had exploited the story to the hilt and the Lindberghs never recovered from the wound.

Though active on corporation boards and a constant round-the-world traveller, Charles Lindbergh was a very private person, not wanting anyone even to write his biography. Honor was restored on April 7, 1954, to the famous Swede from Minnesota when he was made a Brigadier General in the Air Force Reserve.

Lindbergh died of lymphatic cancer on the island of Maui, August 25, 1974. The Rev. John Tincher, a United Methodist pastor from Burlingame, California, held the funeral service the following day, reading these words: "We commit the body of General Charles A. Lindbergh to its final resting place, but his spirit we commend to Almighty God, knowing that death is but a new adventure in existence and remembering how Jesus said upon the cross, 'Father, into Thy hands I commend my spirit'." Lindbergh was inducted into the Scandinavian-American Hall of Fame in 1991 at Minot, North Dakota. A museum has been built in Lindbergh's honor at Little Falls, Minnesota.

CHAPTER 35

Nathan Soderblom –
Swedish Ecumenical Pioneer

WHEN WE MOVED to Webster Groves, Missouri, a suburb of St. Louis, in November 1961, I was expecting to begin doctoral studies at Concordia Seminary while being pastor of Bethany Lutheran Church, a small congregation of Danish background. It was also the intention to give our children the experience of living in a large metropolitan community. As much as we loved the wide open prairies of North Dakota, I believed it would be to their advantage to learn how to live in an urban area.

This was about the time when Pope John XXIII announced the Second Vatican Council to be held in Rome from 1962-1965. Being interested in such events and open to people of other traditions, I decided to learn about it. The Council's agenda was "aggiornamento," a renewal of the Roman Catholic Church which included "ecumenicity." The word "ecumenical" refers to the worldwide promotion of Christian unity and cooperation. It's based on the belief that "oneness" is an essential quality of the Christian faith. Ecumenism was not invented by Vatican II, but it gave it a tremendous boost. The mutual intolerance and standoffish politeness of previous times were no longer to be the pattern of relationships in the Christian world.

Our move to St. Louis couldn't have been at a more fortunate time. Not only did the the ministerial associations promote the ecumenical theme, but the St. Louis Archdiocese extended courtesies to the public never before accorded. His Eminence, Joseph Cardinal Ritter, was particularly gracious. I became acquainted with Msgr. Joseph Baker, Ritter's "peritus" (specialist) in canon law who accompanied him to Rome. As a result, I was frequently invited to speak to Roman Catholic congregations to share with them my understanding of the faith as experienced by a Lutheran Protestant. I was always well received.

The ecumenical impetus had been hastened when Protestant and Roman Catholic clergy were imprisoned together in Nazi concentration camps for opposing Hitler. But one of the earliest ecumenical leaders in modern times was a Swedish Archbishop named Nathan Soderblom (1866-1931). He was born in the province of Halsingland into a pious Lutheran parsonage which gave him a passion for the ministry. His home and the times were influenced by an evangelical revival. There was a great love of music in the home where he learned to play the piano, organ and French horn. Two strong influences on his life were the writings of Albrecht Ritschl (1822-1889), a German theologian and historian, and Martin Luther. He also admired the music of Johan Sebastian Bach.

While attending the University of Uppsala, Soderblom joined a student missionary group. This gave new directions to his life because it led him to understand the international spirit of missions and to become a serious student of science. In 1890 he attended a Christian Student Conference at the home of Dwight L. Moody in Massachusetts. There he met John R. Mott, a great nineteenth century mission leader.

Unlike the ancient Vikings, this modern Swede was committed to world peace. Three principles guided his thinking in this quest. First, he took seriously the words that Jesus was the "Prince of Peace" and that peace was God's will for the world. Second, he believed that peace in the hearts of men had consequences for how they ought to behave. This meant that personal renewal and the promotion of peace belonged together. Third, the church's witness for peace required unity within itself. He believed that the goals of peace and ecumenism are one. The Nobel Peace Prize was awarded to him in 1930.

Soderblom was ordained in 1893 and became a chaplain in an Uppsala mental hospital. The next year he married Anna Forsell and moved to Paris to study at the Sorbonne. He became fluent in French and completed a doctorate in 1901. While there, he ministered to Swedes in France.

His graduate studies completed, Soderblom returned to Uppsala to teach theology at the University. There he formed friendships with Einar Billing, Gustaf Aulen and Anders Nygren, all who became famous theologians and churchmen. During these years, he also worked to establish close ties with the Church of England. This resulted in "intercommunion" being established in 1922. From 1912-1914 he held professorships in both Uppsala and in Leipsig. In 1914, Soderblom became the Archbishop of Uppsala and Primate (head bishop) of Sweden. As Archbishop, he added contemporary music to the Swedish hymnal.

This was the age of some notable international church meetings. Among these were the Lambeth Conferences in England, begun in 1867. There was also a World Student Christian Federation held in Constantinople in 1911. These had a strong influence on Soderblom. He hosted the Stockholm Conference in 1925. This brought Anglican, Orthodox and Protestant Church leaders together to search for ways to bring about Christian unity.

Another project to which he devoted energy was building a chapel to the memory of St. Ansgar on the island of Birka in 1930, celebrating 1,100 years since the first Christian mission began in Sweden.

Soderblom was elected to the Swedish Academy of Sciences in 1921, a highly prestigious honor. In 1931, he gave the famous Gifford lectures in Edinburgh, Scotland. His strenuous work schedule, including writing seven hundred books and articles, took its toll. A few weeks later, he became ill and died a short while later. He was buried in the Uppsala Cathedral, Sweden's most famous church.

Great leaders don't just happen. They travel many roads and learn how to survive testings by fire. This was the case with Soderblom. He was controversial without being arrogant. He was given many honors but did not seek them. He was often criticized by famous contemporaries, but none of them did more to promote the spirit of ecumenism than did this humble scholar and churchman on whose tombstone was inscribed the words of Luke 17:10, "So you also, when you have done all that is commanded, say 'we are unworthy servants, we have only done what was our duty'."

Soderblom thought of himself as an "evangelical-catholic." The term is somewhat popular in our time, but was a rarity in those days. He cited the Swedish translation of the Apostles' Creed which reads, "Den allmaneliga Kristna tron," which means "the universal Christian faith." "Allmaneliga," which means "all mankind" or "universal," is the Swedish equivalent for the Greek word "catholic."

Though the official Vatican response to Soderblom's ecumenical efforts did not meet with a favorable response at the time, Max Pribilla, a Jesuit from Munich, Germany, praised him, saying, "May God resurrect the catholic Soderblom." John XXIII and Vatican II were the answers to his prayer. Nathan Soderblom, the tireless Swedish Archbishop, is a good name to remember during the week of Christian Unity, January 18-25.

CHAPTER 36

My Unforgettable
Swedish Friend

I T WAS FEBRUARY 1964 in St. Louis. The telephone rang, "This is the International Institute calling. There is a young man here from Sweden who is very lonesome. Would you talk with him?" This began an unusual and interesting friendship that has continued ever since.

Elon Eliasson (AY-lon Ay-LEE-a-son) telephones me at unpredictable times. He used to begin: "Dis is da King!" I'd know his voice anywhere and any time. It's unforgettable.

A native of Gothenborg on Sweden's west coast (where Saab automobiles are manufactured), Elon served in the Swedish navy with Ingemar Johansson, former world heavyweight boxing champion (1959-60). They were good friends and had travelled together in China when no Americans were allowed into the country.

I took Elon to our home in Webster Groves (a suburb to the southwest of St. Louis) where he became acquainted with my family. He was a great entertainer. The children had never seen anyone walk on their hands before. Elon had heard a lot about Chicago gangsters, especially Al Capone. It's no wonder he carried a blackjack in his pocket for protection. One can't be too careful in a strange land.

What brought this Swede to the "Gateway City" of America? Elon was trained as a chef in Paris under a famous teacher. His first job in the United States was at the Waldorf Astoria in New York. His sense of adventure brought him to Trader Vics in St. Louis, a famous Polynesian eating place. He wanted to learn English but discovered he was working with twenty-seven Chinese cooks. A friend, Jack Eriksen, now retired in Billings, Montana, was an engineer at the Missouri Athletic Club. He helped Elon get work at the club so he could become Americanized.

One day, Elon asked us to sponsor his fiancee, Norah Gustafson, to America. A few weeks later, I officiated at their wedding. The service was done in both Norwegian and English (Norah's mother was from Norway and I didn't have a Swedish liturgy). Afterwards he said, "I was married twice." The reception was at the Bevo Mill in south St. Louis. They came to church services every Sunday and stayed for dinner at our house. He liked our food, but used to complain that American coffee was too weak. One time he ran it through the filter a second time. They also put on a Swedish dinner for our congregation. It was a beauty.

Later, Elon and Norah operated Gourmet Delight, a delicatessen in White Plains, New York, just above Manhattan. For a few years he was head chef at a private club where Henry Kissinger was a member. He used to bake Nelson Rockefeller's birthday cake. Elon and Norah still live in the northern suburbs of New York City and continue to please people with their culinary skills.

Norah is also a professional food preparer, a specialist in "kaltbord" (cold table). I've been a guest in their home and was treated royally with Scandinavian hospitality. Some day our phone will ring again and it will be my unforgettable Swedish friend, wondering if I'm still alive.

CHAPTER 37

The Swedes Of
Lindsborg, Kansas

I FIRST HEARD ABOUT LINDSBORG, KANSAS, from Bud and Beulah Mattson who live in St. Louis. Both of them graduated from Bethany College in Lindsborg and are proud of it.

The Swedes of Lindsborg are lovers of culture. Each Holy Week, between Palm Sunday and Easter, they put on the "Messiah Festival of Music and Art." The 108th annual event was celebrated in 1989. The first festival was held March 28, 1882, in Bethany Lutheran Church. The eight-day festival is busy all week long with an excellent program. I saw a live telecast of Lindsborg's "Messiah" concert on Public Television in 1986.

Many people return to Lindsborg each year like it's a religious pilgrimage. They meet in the Presser Auditorium on the Bethany College campus which seats 1,900 people. The choir is limited to 400 singers. The orchestra has about sixty members. Soloists come from New York as well as Kansas. Handel's "Messiah" was performed on Palm Sunday and Easter, and Bach's "St. Matthew's Passion" was presented on Good Friday. On Saturday, an organ workshop and concert was held. Tickets for the week's program are modestly priced.

The 1988 celebration was a special event. It honored Dr. Elmer Copley, Conductor of the Bethany Oratorio Society since 1960 and who retired that year. For twenty-nine seasons Dr. Copley has poured his talent and energy into dedicated service to the community. He is Distinguished Professor of Music (Voice) on the Bethany faculty. His choirs have received excellent reviews both in Scandinavia and America. He planned to continue his work in music after retiring from the Bethany faculty.

The Midwest Art Exhibition is a part of the festival. It's the largest in Kansas and has been held since 1900. It is currently being held in the Birger Sandzel Memorial Gallery on the campus of Bethany College.

How did Swedes ever get to Kansas? From the start, Lindsborg was destined to be a center of high quality culture. It was in large part due to people like Olof Olsson who was educated in Sweden to be both a pastor and a church organist. In 1869, at age twenty-eight, he led 250 of his parishioners from Sweden to make their home in America. Over one hundred of them settled in the Smokey River Valley of Kansas. After only six weeks, Olsson organized Bethany Lutheran congregation and became the recognized leader of the community. He wasted no time in becoming an American citizen. Just two weeks after arrival he began the naturalization process to become an "American." A year later he became the superintendent of schools of McPherson County and organized eight grade schools. He was also elected to the state legislature where he sponsored bills to protect immigrants from exploitation on the labor market and to protect farmers from having their land overrun by the great cattle drives from Texas to Abilene.

The Swedish school which later became Bethany College opened its doors in October 1881. Ten students, both boys and girls, were enrolled, but before the year ended there were twenty-seven students. The second year they had three classrooms with five faculty and ninety-two students. The organizer was Carl Swensson, a young seminary graduate only twenty-one years old. Chosen by Olsson, he proved to be an excellent choice. Another great leader at Bethany was J. A. Udden, who later became an eminent geologist, and taught all the classes except religion in the first year. Swedish congregations of Kansas gave support to the school and in its third year (1883), they had a new steam-heated brick and stone building with classrooms, dormitories and a dining room. They offered teacher education, classics and scientific courses, emphasizing both Swedish and English.

The 1880s began as "boom" years in Kansas. Farm land was easily available through the railroads and the Homestead Act. Credit was easy to get and heavy mortgages were common. The rainfall was generous and the crops were abundant on the rich prairie soil.

But as you could guess, the prosperity didn't continue forever. The lean years came. Rainfall failed in 1887 and for several years afterwards. Crop failures brought bank failures. The eastern banks withdrew their loan money. One newspaper cartoon said, "In God we trusted; in Kansas we busted!"

Bethany College which was the center of the community, felt the pinch. The financial support which had been available at the beginning dried up with the drought. As creditors clamored for their mortgage payments, faculty salaries were paid in promissory notes. It got so bad that King Oscar II heard of their plight and asked the churches of Sweden for an offering to help the beleaguered college. Only $809.78 was collected. Swensson never gave up hope. His motto was "morgon blir det battre" (tomorrow will be better).

Meanwhile, the Augustana Synod of Swedish Lutherans began to worry if they had too many schools to support. Their "flagship" was Augustana at Rock Island, Illinois. President Hasselquist may have feared that Bethany would rival the Illinois school for funds during those hard times. Swensson, however, held firm in his insistence that Bethany was a good investment for the Swedes. In 1889, the Bethany Academy became Bethany College and Swensson became its president. Even though they were deeply in debt, he talked the college board into building a dormitory for girls and a four thousand-seat auditorium for the annual "Messiah" presentation. By 1991, there were 334 students in all of its departments, including thirty-three in college studies. We need to remember, however, that even to get a high school diploma in those days was a prestigious achievement. Bethany graduates were no academic slouches. Twenty-one graduates between 1898 and 1902 continued their graduate studies at Yale.

Lindsborg, Kansas, is still full of Swedes and they are proud of their heritage. It's too bad that King Carl XVI Gustaf and Queen Silvia didn't have time to visit this community while they were here for the "New Sweden '88" days. They'd have received a royal welcome. However, if you should drive through Kansas, stop in at Lindsborg and visit with these fine people. They'll treat you like royalty. They're a hardy people to have survived on the prairies while remembering the best of their heritages, both Swedish and American.

If you'd like more information on the Lindsborg Swedes, write to the American-Scandinavian Association of the Great Plains, P.O. Box 265, Lindsborg, Kansas 67456. They publish a periodic newsletter.

CHAPTER 38

Governor Hugo Aronson – Montana's 'Galloping Swede'

T HERE ARE A NUMBER OF PEOPLE that I'd like to have met. Some of them lived before my time. Many lived too far away or for other reasons I've never met them. One of these people is J. Hugo Aronson (1891-1978), born on a ten-acre tenant farm in Gallstad, Sweden, who later became Montana's thirteenth governor.

Life in Sweden was hard in those days. Hugo's family (there were seven of them) lived in a little log cabin high up on a hillside. If people could live on scenery, they would have been "millionaires." They cut wood for heating and cooking. Their property consisted of "two cows, one calf, one pig and a half dozen chickens." The cows were also used to pull the plow. They seldom ate eggs because these were sold to buy coffee, sugar and other needed supplies. He wrote that his mother knitted even when they walked, but "never on Sunday."

Aronson called the thirteenth his lucky day. It was on October 13, 1911, that he left the farm to take a ship from Goteberg to America via England. He had worked for five years to save up enough money for the passage and the $25 cash (a year's wages in Sweden at the time) that was required by immigration authorities for admission to the country. He had few earthly possessions, but he had something more important. It was two points of advice from his father: "Hugo, whatever you do, learn to do well," and "do not make a promise unless you can keep it, and if you don't intend to keep it, don't make it." These words stuck with him for the rest of his life.

For two and a half years after arriving in the United States, Aronson saw the country by travelling in box cars, known as "Side Door Pullmans." Starting out in Massachusetts, he'd take a job for a while and then get on the rails again. On his way west to Seattle, Aronson stopped at Lakota and Sarles, North Dakota, where he did farm work. Sarles is near the Canadian border and he wrote home to his parents that the "farm was so big and the eight-horse team so large that I had to go clear to the Canadian border and turn around in Canada."

After travelling to the West Coast with stops along the way, Aronson decided to head east again. He had no special destination, but kept hopping trains. All went well until the train stopped at Columbus, Montana, about fifty miles west of Billings, when the brakeman ordered him off. He got a job on a farm for thirty dollars a month, but when the farmer saw what a good worker he was, he raised the pay to thirty-five.

One Sunday he was sitting on the bank of the Yellowstone River reflecting on his life. Suddenly he began to tremble and shake, remembering the words of his father, "Hugo, whatever you do, do it well." Not wanting to just be a better bum, he decided to forsake his vagrant ways and make something of his life. He wrote that the experience was like a religious conversion. Then he went and filed on 320 acres on the Wyoming-Montana border. It was September 3, 1915.

Building a twelve by sixteen-foot cabin and borrowing a team of mules from a neighbor, he began proving up his claim. Later he bought a team of horses on credit from an Irish neighbor.

When the United States entered World War I, Aronson tried to convince some of the other young men to sign up. He was turned down by the navy, but was accepted by the army. By December he was on his way for training. The last stop was Camp American University near Washington, D.C. His big disappointment was that he landed in the hospital with mumps and pneumonia while his outfit shipped out. In fact, he cried because he was left behind. On the way over, the ship was torpedoed off the coast of Ireland with a large loss of life.

When the war ended, Aronson married a French girl named Matilda. They lived on his claim in Wyoming until 1923, when they moved to Sunburst, Montana. There he went into the construction business. Oil was booming in that part of Montana, and Aronson was right in the middle of it, building rigs and running trucks. Soon he was on bank boards and had become a community leader. Never afraid of hard work and long hours, he made good money and made several trips back to Europe. On a trip in 1936, Matilda died of cancer. He had gone back there so she could be with her family when she died.

Those were the days he earned the nickname the "Galloping Swede." Aronson was always on the go, never walking but "galloping." He was also a strong booster of community projects. Likewise, he was never too busy to help a person in need and he never forgot a friend.

In 1946 Aronson sold his trucking business, rig building business, and pipe line and general oil field contracting, to take care of his 4,000-acre farm near Cut Bank. He enjoyed operating his D-7 Caterpillar. In 1951, 3,300 acres of wheat were hailed out, figured to be worth a quarter million dollars. Tears were shed, but he didn't dwell on self-pity, instead he went to town and visited with a Presbyterian pastor friend who gave him counselling. He came away a stronger man.

The Native Americans found a good friend in Aronson. He was inducted as a chief into both the Blackfoot tribe of Montana and Kainai (Blood) tribe in Canada. He regularly attended the Indian ceremonies.

It was natural that a person with Aronson's interest in public life should be drawn into politics. He was elected to the Cut Bank City Council in 1934. Four years later he was elected to Montana's House of Representatives. Reluctant to be a candidate because he felt unqualified, having only a limited elementary education in rural Sweden, Aronson said he'd been educated in the "college of hard knocks." He was sure that he'd never have been accepted into politics back in Sweden because of his family's poverty. In 1944, Aronson was elected to the state Senate and served until 1952 when he was elected governor. Also in 1944, he was married to Rose McClure (a Democrat!). He claimed that this helped him win elections. However, she became a staunch Republican. Their only child, Rika, was born on December 13, 1945 – St. Lucia Day in Sweden.

Aronson served as governor for eight years – 1952-1960 – (the Eisenhower years). Being elected as a Republican in Montana meant a tough campaign, as the state is usually Democratic. But a coalition of people from both parties and Independents elected him. Speaking to a joint meeting of the House and Senate, he told them: "Our goal is to do our best for Montana and the nation and to protect the heritage that we have here for our children. There is no place here for partisan politics, sectionalism or special privilege." Having made no campaign promises to individuals, corporations or interest groups, his hands were not tied and he retained the respect even of his political rivals.

As governor, Aronson had a special concern for education since he was deprived of it himself. He liked Ike and hosted the president in Montana in 1954. He also hosted the Governor's Conference in 1959 at Glacier Park. He wanted them to be impressed by the greatness of the state. While governor, he was also invited to Sweden and presented the Grand Cross of the Royal Order of the North Star. This was a highly emotional event for Aronson to think that he, the son of a poor farmer, would receive the highest honor of his native land.

At the recognition dinner in his honor at the close of his governorship, a large number of tributes were paid Aronson, including the heads of government in the United States and Canada. I was impressed by the tribute from Rev. Nels Norbeck, pastor of St. John's Lutheran Church in Helena. He noted that whenever the Governor was home he could be counted on to be in church on Sundays, even if he returned home in the wee hours of the morning. Aronson used to say: "Sometimes in the fishing or hunting season when it's pretty important to be outdoors, one should still try to be in church as much as possible."

God and country received the highest loyalty from Aronson. He wrote that he prayed both morning and evening (in Swedish), as well as while working on the oil fields and in the governor's office. He often expressed deep appreciation for America as this "great country" and for "this great state of Montana."

My favorite story about Aronson was when he was campaigning for governor. He told the people that if elected he would "try to get rid of all the scavenger fish in the lakes and streams of Montana and stock them with Lutfisk!"

CHAPTER 39

Gen. Keithe E. Nelson –
Chief Air Force Lawman

I HAVE A LOT OF FRIENDS AND ACQUAINTANCES who are lawyers, and some are on large city staffs. But none of those legal partnerships compares in size to the firm formerly headed by Gen. Keith E. Nelson, who was the 9th Judge Advocate General of the U.S. Air Force and commander of the Air Force Legal Services Center.

Gen. Nelson was in charge of 1,385 military attorneys, plus two hundred civilian attorneys and approximately 1,100 reserve attorneys. This has to be one of the largest law firms in the world. It functions on more than 160 locations around the globe.

When he entered the University of North Dakota as a transfer student in 1954, Nelson had never planned on an Air Force career. A native of Grand Forks, he graduated from Concordia High School in St. Paul and continued his first year of college in the Twin Cities also at Concordia, an institution owned and operated by the Lutheran Church – Missouri Synod. He had originally planned to become a pastor.

Languages were a special interest to the future Air Force attorney. Two special events crossed Nelson's life while at UND. One was his marriage in 1955 to Shirley Jordahl, also of Grand Forks. The other was joining the ROTC program, required of underclassmen at Land Grant universities at that time. His undergraduate degree in philosophy had to be delayed until he'd completed the ROTC program in 1958. He received his law degree in 1959.

Being married while going to college is nothing new, but Nelson remembers those student days as being pretty busy. During those four years, he held down a full-time job in addition to classes and homework. Three years were spent as a night watchman and janitor at the Vets Club. While doing the janitor duty at night, Nelson could study for three to four hours. Then he went directly to classes and slept in the late afternoons and evenings. He comments, "Naturally, our social life was limited."

But he attributes his success as an Air Force Attorney to the discipline learned in his student days together with the "fine personalized education I received at UND."

The first assignment for the new Air Force lawyer was at Lake Charles, Louisiana. Moving into that hot and humid climate in the summer of 1959 was tough on the young North Dakotan who was accustomed to the mildly warm days and cool night breezes of summer on the northern prairies. January was more welcome than July to the Nelsons while in the South.

Nelson had planned to leave military service after his three year enlistment and return to North Dakota to put up his shingle to practice law. Then he was offered an assignment in Germany if he'd stay an additional year. Nelson says he "jumped at the chance." They liked Europe so well that they stayed there four years. In Germany, they were stationed near Trier, the summer home of the Roman emperors. A number of my Air Force friends who've been stationed in that area have commented about the richness of that area's history.

Looking back on the European assignment, the Nelsons remember the travelling they did with their VW camper. They visited every country in Europe except Albania. Their travels took them from the far north of Norway to North Africa, and from Ireland to Moscow and they made it a point to get acquainted with the people of the land wherever they visited. They became acquainted with the Laplanders of Scandinavia, the nomads of Turkey, the peasants of Romania and the working people behind the "Iron Curtain."

It was still Nelson's dream to return to North Dakota, so he informed the assignment officers that he would return to civilian life in 1965 unless they'd assign him to the Grand Forks Air Base. They must have thought highly of him because Grand Forks was home for the Nelsons during the next four years. He served as Senior Attorney of the Base Legal Office. Those were delightful years as he renewed friendships with the University and colleagues in the state. He also visited Minot for consultation with the Air Force Base.

Nelson again planned to leave military service after another year while at Grand Forks. But then another intervention took place. The senior officer in charge of legal matters for the base was removed. Nelson was named to be the acting head of the department while just a captain with only six years of experience. The commanding officer took a liking to him and intervened to have him appointed to the position permanently, even though a Lieutenant Colonel normally held the job. He spent three years as the Senior Attorney in his hometown. He says, "it could not have been better." 1968 was spent at the Air Command and Staff College in Montgomery, Alabama. There he studied leadership management, geo-politics and military staffing.

The Nelsons spent 1969-1973 at two bases in England. The first year was Wethersfield in Essex. This is near the ancient site of Bury Saint Edmunds, which commemorates one of England's revered kings who came to a violent end in combat with the Vikings. The second year was with the Royal Air Force at Bentwaters near Ipswich in Suffolk. That interested me since Fiske families from Surnadal, Norway, migrated to Suffolk in the Viking period. Nelson encountered the name while there.

The travel was professionally useful too. Nelson became acquainted with many European attorneys, including barristers, solicitors and judges in England. This brought an invitation to Queen Elizabeth's birthday celebration. Attending a royal birthday party required a certain protocol of dress. So he rented a top hat and morning coat with tails. As they walked down the streets of London, looking like "English gentry," tourists photographed them, not realizing that this was an American military family dressed for the Queen's party.

After the assignment to England, Nelson transferred to Washington at the office of Management of Manpower and the Judge Advocates worldwide. During that time, he remembers visiting the Minot AFB in February 1974. He made several more visits to the Minot base. In 1977 Nelson was commandant of the Air Force Judge Advocate General school, commonly known as JAG, at Maxwell AFB in Alabama.

What does an Air Force Judge Advocate General do? Nelson describes his department's job as consisting of "Constitutional issues, environmental law and lawsuits, government contracts, international law, space law, military justice and many other specialized areas of the law." Their staffs have appeared before the bar of many Federal courts, including the United States Supreme Court. He admitted, however, that military life was a "roller coaster." Still, he impressed me as thoroughly enjoying it.

Besides his heavy schedule of Air Force work, Nelson is an avid tennis player. "My racket travels wherever I do," he states. He also enjoys shotgun sports and has done a lot of competition shooting. The busy Air Force attorney still found time to hunt geese. What he especially liked about getting out in the fields was the "solitude of a goose pit and the beauty of one of God's most majestic creatures in flight." Now that he is retired, I suspect Nelson is doing more of his favorite things.

Nelson shared with me some things about his Scandinavian heritage. His father's family emigrated from Sweden and his mother's family from Norway. Minot holds a special place in his heart because his grandfather was a carpenter in the Magic City and this is where his father was born. He's quite excited about his Scandinavian roots and likes to talk about them. His mother's family comes from Christiansand in the south of Norway and his wife's family is from Christiansund (the same place as Hubert Humphrey's mother), on the coast west of Trondheim.

Modern day Scandinavians show up almost everywhere, even in the Pentagon.

CHAPTER 40

The Scandinavians
Meet In Columbus

THERE HAVE BEEN MANY SCANDINAVIAN organizations in America, but none of them as influential as the
church. Despite warnings and threats from the Lutheran
state churches in Scandinavia against going to America,
many immigrants looked to their pastors for leadership in the
New World.

Because they came from different countries, at different times,
and to different places, it was a slow road to unity for the
Scandinavian Lutherans in America. When they finally met for
their great reunion, it took place in Columbus, Ohio, where
Scandinavians are scarce.

A merger of synods with Danish and Norwegian backgrounds
had taken place, together with one of German, in 1960 to form the
American Lutheran Church (ALC). The Lutheran Free Church of
Norwegian background joined the ALC in 1963. In 1962, the
Lutheran Church in America (LCA) was formed by churches of
Danish, Finnish, Swedish backgrounds, together with Germans.

The historic gathering of April 30 - May 3, 1987, united the
ALC, LCA and AELC (Association of Evangelical Lutheran
Congregations) into the Evangelical Lutheran Church in America
(ELCA). The seating arrangements for the 1,045 delegates to the
constituting convention was alphabetical. This meant that they
were integrated from the start and were discouraged from form-
ing power blocks as they voted. I was fortunately seated at a front
row table in the middle of the convention hall. On my left was a
delegate of German background from Dayton and a bishop of
Swedish background from Seattle was on my right.

There's paranoia when mergers take place. I had been a delegate to the constituting convention of 1960 and remember the
fears of that generation. Rumors were floating among the
Norwegians that their leaders had sold out to the Germans and
that congregations would lose their freedom. The Germans in

Ohio were less than happy with moving to Minneapolis to join the Evangelical Lutheran Church of Norwegian origin. I heard some of the same fears again. This would be the "last hurrah" for the Scandinavians before being swallowed up by the German majority. But when it was all over, the Scandinavians went home with the chief executive offices.

Dr. Herbert W. Chilstrom of Minneapolis was chosen to be the Presiding Bishop. He is of Swedish origin with a degree from Augsburg College in Minneapolis, founded by Norwegians. Mrs. Chilstrom is of Norwegian background from Beresford, South Dakota. The newly elected General Secretary was Dr. Lowell Allmen, another Swede.

The headquarters is in Chicago, which has the largest concentration of Scandinavians in America. It's located near the O'Hare Airport so people can fly in for meetings and return the same day to any place in the United States. Just a few miles away is the Lutheran General Medical Center, one of the largest in Chicago, founded by Norwegian Deaconesses in 1902.

It shouldn't be assumed, of course, that all Scandinavians are Lutherans. There have been quite a few Norwegian Methodist and Baptist congregations and a significant number of Swedish Covenant congregations. Once they got over to America, many of them joined whatever denomination was convenient or fit their social status. Some also joined the Mormon trek to Utah in the 1840s. It's a fact of history that the Church of Sweden advised people emigrating to America to join the Episcopal Church rather than the Swedish Augustana Synod because the immigrant pastors had not been ordained in the tradition of "apostolic succession." It's also true that as Scandinavians were moving up the social ladder in America, they often joined one of the "American" churches that fit their new social class.

What took the Scandinavian Lutherans so long to get together? There is no difference in teachings that can be traced to ethnic backgrounds. Scandinavian Lutherans are generally conservative in theology and pietistic in their manner of life. Except for the Finns, they've all understood each other's languages from the time they arrived in America, so language was no serious barrier.

Some people claim it was stubbornness, and I'll have to admit that there is some basis for this. While no race has a corner on self determination, I wouldn't deny that I've met some pretty head-strong Scandinavians who can test the patience of the most pious saints.

One of the speakers at the constituting convention was Dr. Gunnar Staalsett, General Secretary of the Lutheran World Federation from Geneva, Switzerland. Staalsett is a pastor from northern Norway whose grandparents emigrated from Finland. Staalsett took delight in telling us the story of a Norwegian-American woman he met on an airplane. She got right to the point. "I'm opposed to this merger! It's no good," she said. After a pause, she added, "I was also against the last merger (1960), but it worked out alright and I suppose this one will too."

L.GAYLOR

New beginnings in Columbus.

129

CHAPTER 41

1988 – The Year Of
The Swedish-Americans

THE SWEDES WERE THE EARLIEST SCANDINAVIANS to emigrate to the New World after the age of the Vikings. In 1988, King Carl XVI Gustaf and Queen Silvia spent seventeen days in the United States to mark the 350th anniversary of those first Swedes who settled at Wilmington, Delaware, in 1638. A commemorative postage stamp was issued on March 29 to celebrate "New Sweden '88."

Sweden was a power to be feared in the days of King Gustavus II Adolphus (reigned 1611-1632). When he died at the battle of Lutzen, his daughter Kristina ruled from 1632 to 1654. Those were the days when Spain, Portugal, France, Holland and England were looking for places to plant their flags. Sweden also wanted to develop an overseas empire and had short term colonies on the Gold Coast of West Africa and along the eastern American seaboard. It did not last long. Fort Kristina, which is now Wilmington, Delaware, was captured by the Dutch in 1655, who later lost it to the English. The English also took control of the African colony in 1664.

That was the end of the Swedish empire outside of Europe, but Swedish life and influence continued through the churches. It is estimated that there were about 1,500 Swedish settlers and 110 farms in "New Sweden." *Sweden & America*, the publication of the Swedish Council of America (Summer 1987), has identified eight churches that trace their roots back to those days. The most famous of these was Holy Trinity ("Old Swedes") Church in Wilmington. It is still in use and looks about like it did when consecrated in 1699. They still have the original pulpit and silver communion service.

Queen Kristina sent Governor Printz to better organize the colony in 1643 and he moved the seat of government to what is now Essington, Pennsylvania. Their church was named "Gloria Dei," but also nicknamed "Old Swedes." The queen sent the bell and baptismal font which are still being used. Other churches are located around Philadelphia and in Delaware and New Jersey. Originally, these were state churches of Sweden and Swedish speaking pastors were sent by the government to minister to the colonists.

About 1770, when the supply of Swedish Lutheran pastors was no longer available, the congregations became Protestant Episcopal (formerly Anglican), which they still are. This seemed to the Swedish state church clergy the most logical solution to their problem of getting clergy since both the Church of Sweden and the Church of England had "apostolic succession," a direct line of bishops going back to the church of ancient Rome. Those eight congregations worship in English today, but are conscious of their Swedish heritage.

Some famous people lived in "New Sweden." Among them was John Hanson, first president of the American Continental Congress, sometimes called the "first president of the United States." Another was John Morton who signed the Declaration of Independence.

Perhaps the most famous contribution of the early Swedish community was the log cabin. The Swedes and Finns were experts with the use of wood and had developed an ability to cut logs for building fine houses. From the Delaware River valley, the log cabin spread across the whole frontier of America. (There's some debate about the origin of the log cabin in America, but the Swedish claim is well documented.) Seven Swedish log cabins were built on a twenty-five-acre farmstead on the Salem River in New Jersey for the celebration of "New Sweden '88." The craftsmen, using seventeenth century tools, came from Sweden to supervise the construction. The royal family dedicated the New Sweden Farmstead Museum.

I was not surprised a few years ago when visiting Medora, in the Badlands of western North Dakota, to find some Finnish carpenters from northern Minnesota building an addition to the Harold Schaefer log home. Their skill with an axe for cutting logs to size for a building was something to see.

Emigration from Sweden to America did not cease after "New Sweden" became a part of "New Holland" and finally "New England." However, those Swedes, like other Scandinavians, tended to melt into the American scene. After the Civil War, however, when large numbers of Swedes settled in America, they started to preserve their heritage.

The Swedish Council of America, located at 2600 Park Avenue in Minneapolis, is made up of seventy-five-member organizations. This group is doing an unusually fine job of promoting their heritage. The founding members of the Council were the American Swedish Historical Foundation, the American Swedish Institute, the Detroit-Swedish Council and the Swedish Pioneer Historical Society.

His Majesty King Carl XVI Gustaf is the "Patron" of the Council and visited ten major cities in the United States for the celebration of "New Sweden '88." One of the largest celebrations was in Minneapolis. Curtis L. Carlson of Minneapolis, Board Chairman of the Radisson Hotels, was the honorary chairman of the U.S. National Committees for "New Sweden '88." Dr. James M. Kaplan, professor at Moorhead State University (Minnesota), was Chairman for the North Dakota Committee. While the royal family was feted in Minneapolis, Swedes and their friends in Fargo-Moorhead had a dinner with a large TV screen to watch.

There were some special events happening in North Dakota too. The Chautauqua in Devils Lake was dedicated to "New Sweden '88." Money was raised to bring music students from Sweden to the International Peace Garden Music Camp.

The North Dakota Heritage Center in Bismarck had special displays on the Swedes in North Dakota. Swedish artists performed at the University of North Dakota and the Fargo-Moorhead Symphony had a concert of Swedish music. So if you're Swedish, even though 1988 is past, stand tall and let the world know that you're proud of your heritage.

PART III

*The Heritage
Shared With Their
Scandinavian
Neighbors*

CHAPTER 42

Who Are
The Scandinavians?

THE PEOPLE OF FIVE NATIONS make up the Scandinavian heritage. These are: Denmark, Finland, Iceland,
Norway and Sweden. The Scandinavians, however, have
been a traveling people and now live in all parts of the
world. Their greatest concentration is found in the United States
with large numbers in the upper Midwest states and on the East
and West Coast.

The Scandinavian lands, with the exception of Iceland, are
known to have been inhabited since before the last Ice Age.
People have lived in Denmark since at least since B.C. 10,000 and
in Norway, Sweden and Finland since B.C. 8000 Iceland was not
settled until the ninth century A.D., though Irish monks had
arrived two centuries earlier. Iceland was settled by Norwegians
fleeing from the tyranny of King Harald "Haarfager" ("Finehair").
The Icelandic people of today still speak the Old Norse of that
period. The Danes, Norwegians and Swedes are a distinct
Teutonic language group and share a common heritage with the
North Germans and Dutch. This "Germanic" immigration to the
Scandinavian lands began about B.C. 2000 and covered a lengthy
period of time.

There are, of course, no "pure races." In addition to the typically blonde and blue-eyed Scandinavians, there are many with
darker complexion that settled especially in western Norway.
Many flaxen haired Celts were taken as slaves from Ireland and
blended in with the Norwegians. They were given their freedom
after Norway became Christian.

The term "Scandinavia" was originally "Scatinavia," and was a
misspelling in the writings of Pliny the Elder. In A.D. 5, Emperor
Augustus sent his Rhine fleet to explore the region and then it
became forgotten from the pages of history for almost four hundred years.

The people of Finland are a part of a migration that passed through Hungary and Estonia. Because Finland was under Swedish rule from 1362 to 1809, there are many Finns of Swedish origin especially in the southwestern part of the country, around Turku, the old Swedish capital. Swedish is an official language of Finland today, together with Finnish. In 1809, Russia occupied Finland and it did not gain its independence until 1917. The Russians made Finland a "Grand Duchy" and chose Helsinki for their capital. This was closer to St. Petersburg, the home of the Czars.

During the ninth through the eleventh centuries, the Scandinavians spread out in a series of conquests and colonizations to England, Scotland, Ireland, the North Sea islands, Russia and the Baltic areas. They carried on trade in a much larger area and were given possession of that part of France called Normandy ("Northmandy"). If you find some French people with blonde hair and blue eyes, ask if they are "Normans."

But where have all the "Vikings" gone? Are they only in the movies and comic strips? And what kind of people were they really like? These hardy people who knew no fear in war or on the high seas, whose cruelty earned them a fearsome reputation, became eager settlers in the lands where they waged war. Once they became colonists, they became traders instead of raiders. They also became peaceful patriots, often joining in defensive wars against their former countrymen. Though war was a part of their culture, their main interests were trading and finding places to live for the people of their overcrowded homelands. "Primogeniture" was the law of the land. This meant that only the oldest son was entitled to inherit the family farm and other property. He also had to care for his parents for so long as they lived.

In America, the Scandinavian immigrants became fiercely patriotic to the cause of the New World. They were a willing part of the "melting pot." My parents would not speak a word of Norwegian to me. That was left to one of my grandmothers who refused to speak a word of English to anyone. Education was of highest priority to these immigrants. Parents would sacrifice all luxuries and conveniences so that their children could get a high school diploma and a college degree. They also established many fine colleges which are still flourishing. The result was that a high proportion of the Scandinavian immigrant families became leaders in politics, science, education, the church and in the arts.

"Scandinavianism" as a modern movement began after the fall from greatness of the two powers, Denmark and Sweden, early in the nineteenth century. Students led the way. Meeting in Copenhagen, they pledged to be true to each other "in life and in death" in their loyalty "to our great common fatherland." Since the super powers of the day feared the political rise of a Scandinavian kingdom, the alliance was kept in the bounds of culture and trade. There was also a strong nationalism in each country which wanted to support the special interests of each nation.

Peace, not war, is the trademark of the Scandinavians today. This is evident in the fact that the first two Secretary Generals of the United Nations came from Scandinavia, Trygve Lie of Norway and Dag Hamarskjold of Sweden.

Small countries need good memories. The people of Scandinavia learned well how to live as close neighbors to the former Warsaw Pact nations and still preserve their heritage of freedom. It was a long time dream of my family to visit Scandinavia. It was quite a surprise to our children to learn that it was the dream of Scandinavian children to go to America. Without doubt, they are some of the best friends America has in the world. Long live the lands of the Northmen and their children everywhere!

CHAPTER 43

The Early
Norsemen

S CANDINAVIA HAS BEEN INHABITED ever since the glaciers melted about ten thousand years ago. We don't know, however, who those first inhabitants were except that they were hunters and wandering tribesmen. They went north to follow the seasonal migration of the reindeer and other wild game.

About B.C. 2000-2500, agricultural techniques were introduced as migrations of new people of Germanic origins pushed into Denmark, Sweden and Norway. Finland was inhabited by a migration that passed through Hungary and Estonia, except for the Sami (Lapps) who appear to have come from Mongol stock.

Ignored in their isolation of the early days, the Norsemen came to the attention of their neighbors to the south in A.D. 793 when a band of them suddenly appeared in longships at the holy island of Lindisfarne. There they brutally plundered the monastery and returned home to tell about the easy loot available in England. From then on, Christian historians painted a villainous picture of them as heathen terrorists, which in fact many of them were.

But there was another side to these people. Many of them were quite civilized and took no part in piracy on the seas. They were good farmers, skilled artisans in working with cloth, wood, metal and bone carving. They also had a democratic form of government that was ahead of anyone else in their part of the world. For 250 years, these "Vikings" were a dominant force in the North Sea lands, along the coastlands of western Europe and up the rivers of Russia.

What more can we know about these people? Were they a single pure race or did they come from mixed origins? What we know has to be pieced together from many sources: rune stones, archaeology, legends and sagas, language study, numismatics (the study of coins) and educated guesses. Some of our best written records come from the early Icelanders.

Anthropologists identify two types of Norsemen. There were the long-headed (dolichocephalic) people who are tall, blonde and blue-eyed. These are characterized as being adventurous and easy going; and the broad-headed (brachycephalic) people described as conservative, distrustful, dark-haired, quick to become enthusiastic, emotional in politics, religion and personal relationships. While the tall, long-headed, blonde and blue-eyed type are found in large numbers in these lands, Sweden has the highest percentage of the long-headed type and Denmark the fewest. Norway is a more equal mixture of both. One should not, however, be too rigid in drawing character conclusions from these observations.

Not all Norsemen were Vikings. Properly speaking, "Vikings" refers to those who made a profession of trade, piracy and land-taking. These had been northern activities long before the "Viking Age."

Despite their great power, the Roman legions were never able to conquer the Norsemen. They did, however, employ many "Germanic" people as mercenaries and even invited them to settle in the Empire as a buffer against further attacks. The Romans explored the coastlines of this region in A.D. 5, but never attempted to occupy it, so far as we know. The earliest reference to these lands comes from the voyage of Pytheas of Massalia, a Greek geographer, in B.C. 330-300. He described the north coast of Denmark quite accurately.

Between A.D. 400 and 550, over-population led many Norsemen to migrate to England. Originally they were invited to settle there after the Roman legions departed, but once there they came in greater numbers and drove the Celts into what is now Wales. The Angles and Jutes from Denmark and the Saxons from northern Germany took over the land but it returned to heathenism, having been Christian under Roman rule. If you read the Prince Valiant or King Arthur stories, you get a good idea of the struggle between the newcomers from northern Europe and the earlier settlers.

Impressive grave sites from the Merovingian Period (A.D. 550-800) have been found near Oslo and Uppsala. Cremation was their usual way of disposing of bodies before the coming of Christianity. The bodies and goods were burned on a pyre and then covered with mounds.

Those early Norsemen were known by a variety of names to their neighbors. The "Eruli" or "Heruli" seem to have had their original home in southern Jutland. Driven out by the "Dani" ("Danes") about A.D. 200, they invaded Gaul (France) in A.D. 289. Later they plundered the coast of Spain. They were also famous as mercenaries. They are best remembered for their skill at writing with runic characters.

The Roman historian Tacitus paid tribute to the Swedes of about the year A.D. 100 as the more powerful and better organized of the northern nations. In the early days, Scandinavian kings were petty rulers who had small areas under their control. Many battles were fought before any of these lands came under the rule of a single monarch.

One of the most interesting of these ancient kings was Harald Blautand ("Bluetooth") of Denmark. His father was the hardheaded Gorm the "Gamle" (the "Old"). Gorm was the first to rule over all Denmark and was a devotee of the pagan gods to the end. His wife Thyri was Christian. It is speculated that she was descended from an English royal house. She was remembered for her beauty, chastity, wisdom and saintliness, according to Prof. Gwyn Jones from Cardiff, Wales, in his book *A History of the Vikings*. My wife and I visited the burial mounds of Gorm and Thyri at Jelling, Denmark, in 1985. They're each fifty steps high.

Harald was the first king of Denmark to embrace the Christian faith. It's difficult to know, however, how much instruction and conviction lay behind his claim to have "made the Danes Christian." It was possibly a combination of influence from his Christian mother, military pressure from the neighboring German king, Otto I, who was Christian, or the Danes in England who had been converted to the new religion. By being baptized, he protected his southern boundary with Germany which permitted him to wage war in Sweden and make claims in Norway. There have been very few people in positions of power who appear to have acted with pure motivations.

In his old age, Harald fled Denmark to escape attack from his son Svein "Forkbeard." After gaining control of Denmark, Svein conquered England and returned to the paganism of Gorm. But Svein's son, Knut the "Great," became a Christian king of England who is remembered for his saintliness. He became the most powerful ruler in the North Sea lands after defeating Olaf the "Saint" in the Battle of Sticklestad north of Trondheim in 1030.

It's unfortunate that historians have concerned themselves so much with kings, battles and intrigue. I'd like to know much more about the everyday life of common people. There's a trend in our times to tell of the past as "people's history," rather than exclusively as a political and military chronicle. The ancient world was a dangerous place for children. Unless the head of the house approved of a newborn child, it was put out to die. Too many mouths could spell disaster when there was a food shortage. It was not much safer for women and for people low on the economic scale. If we think that morals in our time are in jeopardy, we should not be deluded into supposing that the ancient world was a paradise or even better.

Life has mostly been a struggle for survival. Marriage had little to do with romantic love. It is only in our time that luxuries and plenty have been assumed by the masses to be their right. Our ancestors would have thought they'd reached heaven (or, Valhalla) if they could have seen our age.

CHAPTER 44

'Beowulf' – A Scandinavian Epic Poem

THE WORLD NEVER TIRES OF HEROES or hero worship. The best known of these stories was told by an ancient Greek writer, Homer, in the *Iliad* and the *Odyssey*. *Beowulf* is also such an epic poem about a Scandinavian warrior from Sweden who rescued Denmark from two great monsters and fought a duel unto death with a dragon in his own land. It's the oldest story in a modern European language.

Written in Anglo-Saxon England about the seventh century, it reflects life among the Danes and Geats from a century earlier. The invasions of Britain by the Angles and Jutes from Denmark, and Saxons from northwest Germany, during the fifth and sixth centuries, provided the setting for this story. When the Roman legions left this island early in the fifth century, waves of Teutons poured in as settlers and conquerors. They remembered their homelands just as the Icelandic sagas recorded the deeds of the Norse kings five centuries later, or as modern Scandinavians in America still search for the heroes of their homelands.

Tragedy struck Denmark. Grendel, a man-eating monster, who lived at the bottom of a stench-filled lake, together with his equally dangerous mother and other monsters, was descended from Cain in the Biblical story. Each night, the dreaded beast broke into the castle and carried off warriors for its midnight meal. For twelve years the castle stood empty and in shambles, awaiting its final destruction.

Deliverance came from a young Gothic warrior named Beowulf who lived in southwest Sweden called "Geatland." He was called "stronger than anyone anywhere in this world." With fourteen warriors, he rowed to Denmark to face the dreaded enemy.

Every victory has its price. Grendel devoured one of the great Geats before the mighty Beowulf seized and fought him, barehanded without sword, until the terrible beast, minus an arm, returned to his murky lake abode, mortally wounded. As always, a big feast was held to celebrate the victory and the castle was repaired. Great gifts were lavished upon Beowulf.

Then another terror appeared. Grendel's mother, bent on revenge, came in the dark of night to work havoc on the castle of the Danes. She smashed their weapons and took the king's closest friend as victim for her supper. His head was displayed on a rock for all to see. Beowulf was summoned to the grief-filled castle.

He tracked Grendel's mother to her lair in the foul lake and descended with full armor to do battle. But always before such battles, a full array of speeches was made, boasting of victory before the fight began. His sword proved useless against the beast for his strength was greater than the iron blade and it shattered with the blow. For a moment he was down and about to be struck by the monster's powerful claw. With mighty effort, he arose and took from Grendel's wall a heavy sword, forged by giants. Its maker's magic proved enough. Grendel's mother fell dead. Then our hero finished off Grendel as well.

After rounds of banquets, the Geats returned to their own land, laden with gifts. Years later, another enemy appeared. A mighty dragon flew through the night to bring destruction to the land. Beowulf was now an old man, having ruled for fifty winters, but still was strong and courageous. He advanced with his warriors to the dragon's lair, but at first sight of the beast, they all fled, leaving only Beowulf and Wiglaf, his loyal companion, to face the terror.

The dragon's fire melted his shield and his sword shattered upon striking the beast's scaly coat. Its poisoned tusks found their mark in Beowulf's neck. Then Wiglaf struck a mighty blow to fell the dragon and brought it to its death. Dying, Beowulf gave Wiglaf the kingdom and the treasure from the dragon's den.

A giant funeral pyre was built to burn Beowulf's body. Wiglaf added the dragon's treasure to the fire, since none was worthy to claim it. Difficult days were ahead. News of the king's death would bring war with the Uppsala Swedes, the Frisians and Germans. There was no great warrior to protect their borders and homes.

The fact that cremation, instead of burial, was used is clear evidence that this story was pagan Anglo-Saxon in origin. The minstrel who carried the song is unknown, but language was no barrier then. They spoke a common tongue. The poet who first told it several centuries later was evidently Christian. The frequent references to "Almighty God" are clearly Christian and one would be led to think that Beowulf was such himself. But this can hardly be the case.

Is this history or romantic fiction? Higlac, an uncle of Beowulf and king of the Geats, is mentioned by Gregory of Tours in his *History of the Franks*. Beowulf was most likely a mythical person who never lived, but embodied the ancient ideal warrior, like St. George, who fought with the enemies of mankind to make the world safe. A delightful translation of Beowulf was printed by Alan Sutton Publishing, Wolfboro, New Hampshire (1988) and was performed on stage in a London Theatre in 1981 by Julian Glover. The introduction was written by Magnus Magnusson.

Our age is not so eager to glorify warriors and approve the ways of violence. We abhor it and yet violence itself has increased. Times will change, however, and the warrior hero may again return to receive his due.

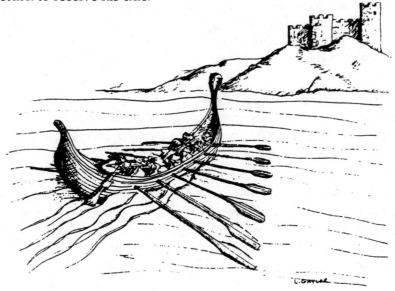

Beowulf goes to Denmark.

CHAPTER 45

The Volsunga –
National Epic Of The Northmen

OLD STORIES NEVER DIE, but they may take new shape and form. The Volsunga saga is such a literary creation. This national epic of the Scandinavians, British and Germans, even found its way into the story of Beowulf (A.D. 675-725). The Volsunga saga is the story of the Volsungs and Nibulungs which belong to the early legends common to the northern world.

The Icelanders wrote this saga about the year 1200. It furnished the background for Richard Wagner's opera "The Ring of the Nibelung." The entire opera was premiered at the Metropolitan Opera in New York in March 1889. The first of the four cycles, "The Rhinegold," had been performed in Munich twenty years earlier. Wagner's opera has a cycle of four musical dramas which still draws excited crowds to its performances of heavy Germanic music fitting to the story.

The two outstanding characters in the story are Sigurd (also spelled Siegfried) and Brynhild (also spelled Brunhild). Sigurd's father, Sigmund, was a mighty warrior of the Volsung family descended from Odin, the "All-Father" god of the Norsemen. Because Sigmund was killed before Sigurd's birth, his mother, Hjordis, married Alf, the king of Denmark. Sigurd grew up as a handsome warrior, full of wisdom and courage, with a head of heavy blonde hair. He mastered the skills of blacksmithing, music, carving runes, learned several languages and was eloquent in speech – the basic attributes of a Scandinavian warrior.

As Sigurd reached manhood, his friend Regin urged him to ask King Alf for a war-horse. He found one that was a descendant of Sleipner, Odin's eight-footed steed, fabled in the sagas.

Every good story has to have a conspiracy at its heart. Even the Gospels have such a theme. Regin's father, Hreidmar, had become very rich with gold. He was the envy not only of political rivals and the gods, but also of his sons. Greed for gold has been the undoing of many people. Fafnir, the oldest son, murdered his father to claim the treasure. Then he changed himself into a dragon to guard his hoard from Regin.

Fleeing for his life Regin found Sigurd and convinced him to avenge his wrongs by slaying the dragon. For this task, Sigurd needed a sword worthy of the deed. The fragments of Sigmund's sword were forged so skillfully that it split the anvil without even suffering a scratch. Sigurd was now ready to challenge the dragon, Fafnir.

The struggle with the dragon recalls Beowulf and St. George, both of whom had slain dragons. The Volsung saga tells the story of the battle with the same concern for details as Wagner's opera, "The Valkyrie." The struggle took Sigurd into the dragon's cave. As the slimy dragon moved to his watering place, Sigurd delivered the death blow by thrusting his sword under Fafnir's left shoulder.

As in an opera where dying takes a long time, there was an extended conversation between Sigurd and the dragon. After the death blow, Fafnir, who had been a mighty warrior before turning himself into a dragon, wanted to find out all there was to know about his slayer. Finally, Fafnir tells him to get on his horse and ride with haste to find the gold.

At this point Regin became surly and jealous, being afraid to lose the treasure to Sigurd. Feigning friendship, he asked Sigurd to roast the dragon's heart on a spit for him to eat. Suspecting nothing, Sigurd carried out the request. In touching it to see if it was tender, Sigurd burned his fingers so severely that he put them in his mouth. As soon as the dragon's blood touched his lips, Sigurd was able to understand the language of the birds. That's how he learned that Regin was planning to kill him. Whereupon Sigurd slew Regin.

Sigurd's greatest challenge was yet to come. He found a beautiful warrior-maiden fast asleep on a mountain. With great effort he woke Brynhild and it was love at first sight. She was a goddess who had been banned to the world of mortals. They were married, but did not live happily ever after. In the stories of mythology and in operas, as also in real life, fate frustrates the best laid plans.

Sigurd went off to do more battles. Having been bewitched, he forgot the beautiful Brynhild and sought the hand of Gudrun in the land of the Niblungs. She was the "most beautiful of maidens" in the land. An alliance of blood was sealed between Sigurd and the Nibelungs. During the wedding feast, Sigurd gave his bride some of Fafnir's heart to eat. The moment she tasted it her nature changed to become cold and silent.

Gudron's eldest brother, Gunnar, became king of the Nibelungs. Since he was not married, his mother counseled him to seek the hand of Brynhild who had been left with family but no husband. There was, however, a ring of fire around her house. She had vowed that she would marry only the warrior that dared to brave the flames. Sigurd, having forgotten Brynhild, went with Gunnar. However, the horse would not ride through the flames. So Sigurd and Gunnar changed armor and it was Sigurd who rode through the fire disguised as Gunnar. This is perfect story material for an opera.

The surprised Brynhild agreed to the marriage and promised to appear in ten days for the wedding. During the ceremony, the spell that had been cast over them was broken. But it was too late. The vows had been made. Brynhild's warrior spirit returned and her heart was fierce with anger. The two queens, Brynhild and Gudron, became bitter enemies. Gudron then produced the ring that had originally been given to Brynhild by Sigurd. Brynhild became full of anger from frustrated love and anger and she conspired Sigurd's death.

In Wagner's opera, the death scenes are even more dramatic. Brynhild, mounted on her horse, leaped from the flames and led her battle-maidens back to Valhalla (heaven), passing forever from the sight of earth and men. In a short time, Sigurd died and Gudron fled to the home of King Alf where she spent the rest of her life embroidering the great deeds of Sigurd on a tapestry, and attending her daughter Swanhild who reminded her of the great Sigurd.

In those days when people didn't have theater and television, they found entertainment and philosophy of life in the sagas. Strange as they are to us, and often horror-filled, these stories are probably no more tragic than the world in which we live today. We may not turn ourselves into dragons and cast spells on our enemies, but we try every form of magic at our command to get the best of each other. Some day, a saga may be written about us and an opera about our times. I wonder what they will say and what kind of music they will play.

Sigurd Volsunga

CHAPTER 46

The Great
Viking 'Breakout'

THE SCANDINAVIAN PEOPLE were in serious trouble 1,200 years ago. They needed land. But where would they go? They couldn't move south because the kingdom of the Franks and their powerful ruler, Charlemagne, controlled the main part of the continent. As long as he lived, they were effectively blocked from southern expansion. He died in 814.

The chronist, Adam of Bremen (d. 1081), wrote of the Vikings in the tenth century that "forced by the poverty of their homeland they venture far into the world to bring back from their raids the goods which other countries so plentifully produce." Another chronicler wrote, "great armies of Norsemen like storm-clouds or swarms of grasshoppers" descended upon their countries.

The Vikings were experts in detecting weaknesses in their enemies, so they attacked where they had a chance of winning. The Danes swept into Frisia (Holland), southern England and northwest France. The Norwegians moved into the Orkney and Shetland Islands, the Isle of Man off the southwest coast of England, Ireland, Scotland, northeast England, Iceland and Greenland. They didn't stop until they reached the eastern coasts of North America. The Swedes went east into the Baltic regions (Latvia, Estonia and Lithuania), into northwest Russia and down its mighty rivers until they came to the gates of Constantinople.

What gave them such energy and what made the "breakout" impossible to stop by their neighboring lands? Having been isolated from the main currents of European society, they developed their own civilization. They broke out in their longships and moved up into shallow creeks and hidden estuaries. They could strike quickly on unsuspecting victims. That's why they were called "Vikings." The word "vik" is derived from the word "bay." The word was later found in the vocabulary of the Algonquin Indians of eastern United States.

Barbarians (literally, those who could not speak Greek, the cultural language of civilization two thousand years ago) normally have had a military advantage over people who have become comfortable in their culture. The so-called "civilized" people forget that the "barbarians" didn't live by the same set of values and were not above using treachery. As a result the Germanic tribes finally broke through the defenses of the Roman Empire. The English and Irish, who had become comparatively gentle people under Christian influence, were completely unprepared for the onslaught of the raiders from the North.

The Swedes went east and established trading communities in Finland, the Baltic lands and Russia. Their goal was Constantinople, the capital of the Roman Empire of the east. While never conquering it, they did force the emperor to trade with them and they served as his palace guard. They also gave their name "Rus" to the land. It's from a Finnish word "Ruotsi," which means "rowing men." In the Ukraine they were invited to organize the first government in Russia (a claim challenged by Soviet historians). Like the other Norsemen who had gone into western Europe, they eventually melted into the native populations. In each case of expansion, they began as raiders but ended up as colonists and traders.

The Norwegians found the green hills of Ireland much more to their liking than the rocky fjords back home. They controlled every river and stream with their longboats and built Ireland's first cities. Prior to their coming, the Irish communities – after Christianity came – were organized around monasteries. And being businessmen at heart, the Norwegians minted coins and traded with other countries. Eventually, they accepted the Christian faith and settled down to be farmers. But since they brought their families and livestock with them, they maintained a separate identity for three hundred years on the Emerald Island. The Norwegians also controlled northeast England and moved from Ireland into northern Wales.

The Danes concentrated on southeastern England and Normandy in France. Normandy was so named because of the Normen (northmen). The Danes had their greatest impact in

England. They too accepted the Christian faith in these lands and brought the new faith back to their homelands.

Despite their reputation as "barbarians," they brought with them a long history of democracy. Though they didn't have a concept of "nationhood" like the one which governed remnants of the Roman Empire, they operated by consensus rather than hierarchial structure. When an envoy of the king of France met to parlay with them, he asked, "Who is your leader?" They replied, "We are all equals." Seeing they had come with great fleets of hundreds of longships, he was astounded that no single leader claimed to be in charge of the operation.

Their laws were derived from the decisions of the "Thing," an assembly of landowning free men. Each district had its own assembly and the judgments of the Things were passed on orally from one generation to the next. They also had regional assemblies where representatives of the local assemblies met, usually in the summer. There they considered such matters as the election of kings, declaration of war and matters of religion. In Iceland these assemblies continued without interruption until 1798. The weakness of their system was that they had no executive branch of government to enforce their laws. As a result many of the individual complaints were settled by duels or other violent means.

Their democratic form of government didn't have an imperial view of nationhood, nor did they always have fixed borders between countries. They operated tribally. One time the Norwegians and Danes fought a fierce battle in Ireland.

Another feature of the Norsemen which showed that they really had a civilization, though vastly different from their neighbors, was their respect for women. Women were held in the highest esteem by the Norsemen and enjoyed rights of property and status unknown elsewhere until many centuries later.

The Normans, who settled in northwest France, learned French manners, customs and the French style of warfare. They also provided France's most vigorous leadership in military, statesmanship, law and religion. They ruled southern Italy and Sicily – their kingdom of the two Sicilies endured one hundred years and once they rescued the Pope from German invaders.

THE HERITAGE SHARED WITH THEIR SCANDINAVIAN NEIGHBORS

When Duke William of Normandy invaded England, he faced a strong ruler, Harald Godwinson, who was his relative. Harald did not lack leadership qualities or courage in facing the invasion. However, he had to march his soldiers 150 miles in five days after a fierce battle at Stamford Bridge in Northumbria with the Norwegian king, Harald Haardraade, the most powerful warrior of his time. The Norwegians were defeated after being caught napping and taken by surprise.

When Harald Godwinson arrived in 1066, to face William at Hastings, he was outclassed by a relatively small invasion force of twelve thousand. But the invaders were equipped with the most modern methods of warfare, cavalry and archers. Struck by an arrow, Harald was killed and his soldiers broke rank.

Individual courage and charisma may go a long way, but it's only when strength is organized that it's effective. It's teamwork, coupled with technology, that wins battles and builds communities. The Normans went on to change England by introducing uniform national laws, fixed taxes and a military loyal to the king rather than to local chieftains. The Vikings (the "bay men") disappeared from history and went back into their geographical isolation. Their passion for democracy never died, however, but emerged in the nineteenth century. This time as advocates of peace.

CHAPTER 47

The Mystery
Of 'Sutton Hoo'

URING THE SUMMER OF 1939 the attention of the world was fixed on the German Wehrmacht, Hitler's war machine. As a result, the greatest archaeological discovery in England's history was overshadowed by the opening shots of World War II. When the war ended almost six years later, Europe was too preoccupied with rebuilding itself to be concerned about the ancient treasure at Sutton Hoo in Suffolk County of eastern England. The treasure is now in the British Museum.

The impression of a wooden ship had been discovered in the sandy soil of an earthen mound. An excavation in July, 1939, revealed that there had indeed been a ship buried there, but all the wood had decomposed; only the iron nails were in place. The probability is that it was a burial ship dating to about A.D. 625. The jewels and armor found at the site made it the richest treasure ever uncovered in Europe. But whose treasure had it been? Was someone buried in the ship and if so, who? Scholars are still searching for the answers.

People who are interested in Scandinavian heritage sooner or later have to deal with the "English connection." The whole North Sea was the world of the travel-minded Norsemen, and England was one of their favorite stopping places. Even today, many Danes and Norwegians go to London for their shopping. The north Germans and the English were rivals to obtain the rights to Bergen as a trade center for their merchandise in the late Middle Ages.

Suffolk County had been attractive to Scandinavians long before the Viking Age (793-1066). During the migrations of the 5th and 6th centuries from southern Denmark and northwest Germany, the Angles, Jutes and Saxons came in such large numbers that they eventually dominated the culture of Britain and gave it a new name "Angle-land" (England). A similar "mass migration" occurred during the large nineteenth century movement of Scandinavians to America. When the letters from America came back to the homeland, thousands more got "America Fever" and sailed westward. The lure of "land for the asking" was irresistible.

The ship discovered at Sutton Hoo is considered to be a forerunner of the later Viking longships that were used so successfully during the period of their power. The armor found in the ship appears to have come from Sweden. Burial in such ships was common in Sweden for royalty and aristocrats during the Anglo-Saxon period.

But who might have been buried at Sutton Hoo? One theory is that it was Raedwald (ruled 599-624), a king who was descended from the Wuffingas ("Wolf-people"). The Wuffingas had come from Sweden and took their name from Wuffa, who ruled from 571 to 578 and was the founder of the dynasty. His father, Wehha, was the first of the East Angles to rule in England. This royal family continued to supply rulers in England until the death of King Edmund in 930. The claim is also made that the Wuffingas had been royalty in Sweden and may have come from the royal house of Uppsala. There were always more royalty than there were kingdoms so that may have motivated them to try their luck in England.

There are some problems, however, in resolving the mystery. The main one is that no body was found. Scientific tests of the soil in the middle of the ship near the armor revealed no trace of human remains in the soil, though there was a high phosphate content near the sword. The phosphate may have come from the remains of an ivory chess set, however. Acid in the sand which covered the ship may have dissolved all traces of bones and teeth.

Another suggestion is that the "Sutton Hoo man" was not buried there at all. He may have been entombed at some other place and the ship could have been simply a memorial to him. Michael Wood, in his book *In Search of the Dark Ages*, believes that a body had been buried there but somehow it disappeared. If the body belonged to Raedwald, what happened to it? Raedwald had been converted to the Christian faith and was baptized, but he recanted when his wife urged him to abandon the new faith. They then compromised and had both a Christian and a pagan altar in their private chapel. The relevance of all of this to the mystery at hand is that some people think his body may have been moved from the pagan mound and given a secret Christian burial.

One of the interesting artifacts found in the ship was a highly ornamented whetstone which could have been used to sharpen the owner's sword. It measures almost three feet long. Since the whetstone had never been used, it may have been a part of the ceremonial equipment to accompany him on the journey to Valhalla. These sceptres were frequently found in Swedish burials. The circumstantial evidence indicates that it was probably a king who had been buried and Raedwald seems to fit the picture.

In addition to jewelry, many coins were also found at the site. They were not dated like ours are today, but it has been determined that they were minted between 620 and 640.

It is said that King Henry VIII had his agents dig for treasure in the Sutton Hoo area. Queen Elizabeth's magician, John Dee, had opened one of the many mounds in the area. Later archaeological digs discovered one of their tools as well as their snacks left behind. It is further said that a gold crown weighing sixty ounces was discovered in the area, but it was sold and melted down.

The archaeologists finished their work on August 23, just nine days before Hitler plunged the world into war. They had found a treasure that had previously only been hinted at in myths, sagas and in the epic *Beowulf*. It was not known that this kind of splendor had existed at such an early time in England. The extent of the find was enormous: a helmet, a sword inlaid with gold and jewels, the whetstone, spears, a battle-axe, a decorated shield, silver drinking horns, silver bowls, silver spoons, a large bowl bearing the stamp of the Empress Anastasius in Constantinople, a gold buckle, coins and more things of value.

There was also an iron stand, sixty-six inches tall, which some scholars think could have been a royal standard to carry the king's banners. Such banners were carried in procession to announce the arrival of the king to a community.

Perhaps we'll learn more. Seventeen mounds have been identified in the area and some have still not been excavated. The mystery of Sutton Hoo may be with us for quite a while, but it does add to our knowledge of the English connection for early Scandinavians. Someday I'd like to explore it for myself.

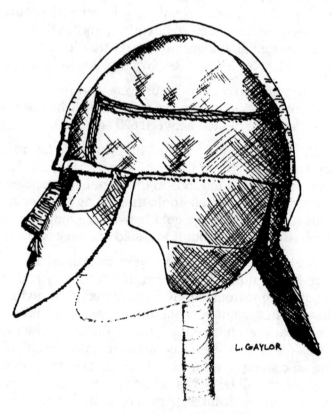

Helmet found at Sutton Hoo.

CHAPTER 48

How Scandinavia
Became Christian

THE STRUGGLE BETWEEN GOOD AND EVIL in our world has many surprises. Who would have guessed that the descendants of the ancient Vikings, once the terror of the Christian world, would become the sponsors of the "Peace Prize" in our time?

A great deal of mystery surrounds the beginnings of those fury-filled bandits of the North Sea lands. On Easter Sunday, A.D. 617, they descended on the Island of Eigg off the coast of Scotland and massacred the fifty-four monks who lived there. For the next five hundred years, no one would live in safety from their raids. The greatest outrage came on June 8, 793, when they sacked the holy island of Lindisfarne, off the northeast coast of England. Shockwaves were felt in the courts of Emperor Charlemagne in France.

The first missionary of distinction to make inroads into these lands was St. Ansgar who had come from France. He made significant beginnings as the missionary Archbishop of Bremen before he died in 865.

England set the stage for the Christian assault on the Viking lands. Much credit has to go to one of its most famous kings, Alfred the Great, for saving his land from the onslaught of the pagan Danes. Combining Christian learning and brilliant military skills, he defeated the Danes and then peacefully persuaded their general, Guthrum, to be baptized in 878. Alfred stood as godfather at the ceremony. From England, the new faith spread back to Denmark. It took a while, but in 965 King Harald "Bluetooth" declared Denmark to be a Christian nation. A stone marked with runic carvings testifies to his words at Jelling in Jutland. My wife and I made a visit to see it in 1985.

It was the story of the "strong Christ" rather than the "gentle Jesus" that converted the Northmen. The Vikings were not a happy people, as we might have supposed. Harsh climate, scarcity of food and the tyranny of pagan gods filled their lives with fear. The Christ whose voice commanded the sea waves and who healed the lepers gave them a new hope. The brutality in their plundering stemmed from the pent up rage which they felt against these forces. "Pity," for the first time, entered their society.

Norway was more obstinate to the missionaries than Denmark. It was the relentless striving of the English bishops that moved two kings named Haakon and two kings named Olaf back to Norway on missionary crusades. The claims of Bishop Grimkel, who promoted the "St. Olaf" legend, completed the turn of events which won the day for the "White Christ."

King Olaf Erickson of Sweden, influenced by a martyred monk from Glastonbury, led Sweden into Christian ways. Finland was reached through Bishop Henry, also English, who had spent time in Sweden. He was martyred on January 19, 1156. Iceland's decision to be Christian was made by a pagan Law-Giver, who decided it would be best for the land. He might have been "influenced" by the fear of Norway's King Olaf Tryggvason.

It touched my heart deeply to see the headquarters of the Nobel Peace Prize in Oslo, knowing that in Norway more blood was shed for the conversion of a nation than anywhere else in Scandinavia. I still believe in miracles.

A statue from Gausdal Church, Oppland.

162

CHAPTER 49

Art In The
Viking World

THE "VIKING WORLD" LASTED for almost 300 years, from 793-1066 A.D. Though the age began in violence, the Vikings have left us a legacy in art which still remains a wonder. From Ireland to Russia and from North Cape to Sicily, Viking skills have influenced art and some of the finest European works of art.

Those were brutal times all over the world. The most civilized culture among Christians was perhaps in Ireland, known as a land of scholars, saints and kings. Islam, at that time, was developing a very high level of culture in art and philosophy. The Vikings, despite their reputation for cruelty, were victims of bad press. The only contemporary writings about them were done by enemies who pictured them as "savages." They were, however, also a highly skilled people who had their own indigenous art forms. A helpful book on this subject is *Viking Art* by David M. Wilson of the British Museum and Ole Klindt-Jensen from the Institute of Archaeology, Moesgaard, Denmark, published by University of Minnesota Press (1980).

Animal ornamentation was known as early as the fourth century A.D. in Scandinavia. Naturalistic art with plant ornamentation was introduced from other parts of Europe. Lions, snakes, horses, deer, dogs and human masks were common to early Scandinavian art. The finest example of the pre-Viking art is the Oseberg ship found near Tonsberg, south of Oslo in 1904. It was covered by a mound twenty feet high and 130 feet long. Hidden beneath was a royal burial. You can see the artifacts at the Viking Ship Museum at Bygdøy Park in Oslo. Besides the well preserved longship, there was a four-wheeled cart, four sledges and utensils. The woman buried in the boat was possibly the mother of King Halfdan the Black. Buried with her was a slave girl sacrificed for the burial. Skeletons of fourteen horses, three dogs and an ox were also found.

The most impressive art is the carving on the prow and stern-post of the ship. Built of oak, the sixty-six foot boat had oar-locks for thirty oarsmen. The wood carving decorated even the bed-posts. The Oseberg must have been one of the finest ships of its time. It reveals a treasure of wood carving, the finest from any Scandinavian period.

In the Viking period, five styles of art are identified. Each was named from the place where examples were found. In the early part of this period, two styles dominated, the "Borre" and the "Jellinge." The Borre style came from a few miles north of Oseberg. As a successor to the art of the famed burial ground, it also included metal work and is identified with a ribbon plait on the borders. The art designs were not limited to the place from which they are named. It is possible to find the Borre style in Sweden, Russia or in Denmark. In this style, the animal head often has a triangular shape and wears a mask.

The Jellinge style takes its name from the most famous burial ground in Denmark. Jelling, northwest of Vejle in Jutland, has two large burial mounds built by King Harald "Bluetooth" for his parents, Gorm and Thyra. The style, however, is found in diverse places. Harald led Denmark into Christianity and these art forms have representations of the crucifixion together with the lion, horse and snake ribbon forms. It bares close resemblances to the Borre style.

Closely related to the Jellinge style is the "Mammen" style from Mammen in Jutland. Strangely, the most famous art pieces at Jelling are claimed to be in the Mammen style. These are the two runestones erected by King Harald. Stone art must have been learned in England by the Danes. They then applied their wood carving patterns to stone. As a result, sometimes Anglo-Saxon and Viking motifs are combined. The Danes occupied a large part of eastern England (Derby, Stamford, Nottingham, Lincoln, Leicester and Yorkshire) called "Danelaw." Norwegians from Ireland occupied a large part of northwest England (Cumberland, Westmorland, Cheshire, Lancashire, Dumfries, West Yorkshire and North Wales). Christian influences are found in art from these regions. England, being a Viking country, produced a great deal of Viking art.

164

The "Ringerike" style comes from a few miles north of Oslo. It features animals with double contours, spiral hips and acanthus-like tendrils. It seems to have drawn a great deal from the Jellinge style.

The "Urnes" style takes its name from a stave church in the Sogn region of western Norway. It frequently features a "combat" motif where the animals bite each other. It is thought that this style may have had its origins in Sweden. It dominated the whole of Scandinavia in the late Viking period and seems to have been promoted by the Normans after their conquest of England in 1066. Its latest development was in Ireland during the twelfth century, when it was dying in Scandinavia.

Viking art was at its best in the use of wood and often found its expression in furniture making. Woodcarving is one of the oldest art forms of Scandinavia. This art affected all levels of society, from the king to the peasant.

Norse Woodcarving –
"The Fiddler."

CHAPTER 50

The Vikings
In Russia

IT WAS MAINLY THE SWEDISH VIKINGS that travelled the rivers of Russia. In fact, "Russia" was once known as "Greater Sweden." The "Rus" of the Viking Age were Scandinavians. They were also known as "Varangians."

A great deal of mystery enshrouds the sagas of the Vikings in Russia. The traditional view has been based on the *Russian Primary Chronicle*, written during the twelfth century in a monastery near Kiev. Although Swedish travel and trade began at least by 650, it was about 860 when the "Rus" were invited to Russia by the leaders of Kiev. The *Chronicle* states: "Let us find a king to rule over us and make judgments according to the law, for our land is large and rich, but there is no order in it. So come and be king over us."

One of those who came was Rurik. He is identified with the founding of Novgorod. The Hermitage Museum in Leningrad, once the Winter Palace of the Czars, has a large collection of Viking artifacts. There is no doubt that Vikings were in Russia. But what did they do and how important were their contributions?

In addition to Russian and Scandinavian records, there were also contemporary Arab accounts. Ibn Fadlan wrote: "I have seen the Rus as they come on their merchant journeys, and stay encamped on the Volga. I have never seen more perfect specimens, tall as date palms, blonde and ruddy. Each man has an axe, a sword and a knife which he keeps by him at all times. Each woman wears neck rings of gold and silver, one for each thousand dinars her master owns." An Arab geographer, Ibn Rustah, described the Rus as traders in furs and slaves. He noted that they wore clean clothing and were hospitable to strangers. He was shocked, however, at their funeral practice of burying alive the favorite wife of a chief with him in his grave.

THE HERITAGE SHARED WITH THEIR SCANDINAVIAN NEIGHBORS

Unlike the Danes and Norwegians who settled as farmers in England, Ireland and France, the Swedes in Russia were interested primarily in trade. One of the great Rus leaders in Kiev was Oleg. In 907, he attacked Constantinople and forced the Greek Emperor to make a treaty giving the Rus trade advantages, including entry visas, customs duties and access to markets and supplies. He also got the Greeks to agree that the Rus should be given as many free baths as they wanted. Despite their bad press, the Scandinavians were a clean living race.

The best known of the Rus leaders was Vladimir ("Valdemar"), the first Christian ruler of Russia and the grandson of Rurik. With help from Scandinavian allies, he conquered his rivals and consolidated a Russian kingdom stretching from Poland to the Volga.

In 988, while Sweden was still pagan, Vladimir converted to Christianity when he married Anna, sister to the Greek emperor. It is significant that he made the Slavic language official for church use, rather than Greek or Scandinavian. This made Christianity a "native" rather than a "foreign" religion.

There was a close relationship between Scandinavia and Russia in those days. Both King Olaf Trygvesson and Olaf Haraldson (St. Olaf) spent times as exiles in Russia. Vladimir is honored not only in the Russian Orthodox Church, but is also listed on July 15 (the day of his death) on the calendar of festivals in the *Lutheran Book of Worship*.

His conversion to Christianity was uncompromising. He put away his eight hundred mistresses, destroyed his idols and became a great builder of churches. Kiev alone had 350 churches. It is perhaps not strange that he died in a battle in which his former wives and their sons rose up against him in 1015.

As time went on, the Vikings in Russia accepted the native Slavic customs. They have done the same in England, France, Ireland, Italy and also in America. The last famous Scandinavian ruler of Russia was Yaroslav who built its first cathedral, St. Sophia, modelled after the famous church in Constantinople.

You should know, however, that the historians of the former Soviet Union had a different interpretation of the importance of the Norse presence. A famous Moscow archaeologist stated: "The role of the Vikings in the formation of the Russian State was rather small." It may be that the western view is glossed with some romantic mythology. There are those, however, who interpret this "downplay" as typical Soviet revisionism and Slavic chauvinism. But in any case, the Viking saga in Russia is made more fascinating by the mystery which surrounds it.

CHAPTER 51

The 'Varangians' In The Emperor's Court

IN THE WORLD OF A THOUSAND YEARS AGO, no city was as exciting as Constantinople. It was the center of trade, culture and political intrigue. The Byzantine Empire, as it was called, was based on the belief that it was an earthly copy of the Kingdom of Heaven. Just as God ruled in heaven, the Emperor was to rule the earth and carry out his commands. Byzantium was no democracy, but rather a rigid autocracy in which the will of the Emperor was supreme. It was the dream of every traveller to visit the city which called itself the "second Rome."

The Vikings were there too. They were known as "Varangians," another name for Scandinavians in that part of the world. It was natural that the exotic tales of this city would fire the imaginations of people as far away as Iceland. Anyone who made such a trip and brought home souvenirs was a hero in his homeland.

The Swedes pioneered the travel routes across Russia down into those lands. Their name for Constantinople was "Mikligardur," the "Great City." They came first as traders and later as warriors. Magnus Magnuson calls those Vikings the "super-technocrats of their time." They led the world in metalwork and ship building. They also had a quick eye on how to make money. The modern name "Russia" was actually another name for Sweden. In those days, Russia was called "Greater Sweden." Once having settled in the cities along the Russian rivers and having built others (for example, Novgorod), they pushed down by the thousands to attack the heavily fortified Constantinople.

The Varangians came to trade in furs and slaves. They forced the Emperor to give them these rights. It was not long before they had won a place in the Emperor's court as the "palace guard." Powerful monarchs were always eager to hire mercenaries. The Vikings became the Emperor's elite "enforcers." Emperor Basil II, who came to power in 976, made the Swedes from Russia into a separate regiment of "life-guards." Even Chinese writers, who visited the "Great City," told about "the tall, blue-eyed, red-haired men" that they had seen. While most of the Varangians were Swedes, many Norwegians were also "soldiers of fortune" among them. They were often given the tasks which were not for the "nice minded."

The military had the highest priority in the Byzantine government. Discipline was extremely severe. Flogging and cutting off the nose or ears was standard punishment for disobedience or cowardice, as well as blinding and execution. An unlucky general might be paraded through the city on a donkey dressed in women's clothes as a mark of shame and disgrace. The Varangians had their own officers that were responsible to the Emperor for which they were paid a salary. "Plunder" was one one of the benefits of a military campaign. The Emperor took one seventh, the officers took half of the balance and the rest was given to the soldiers. As you can guess, there would be cheating. The greatest of all the Varangians was Harald "Hardrada," a half-brother of "St. Olaf," who returned to Norway and later died invading England in 1066.

CHAPTER 52

The End Of
The Viking Age

THE "VIKING AGE" BEGAN IN 793, according to many historians, when Norwegian fortune hunters ravished the Christian holy island of Lindisfarne off the northeast coast of England. It ended at the battle of Stamford Bridge in October 1066 when King Harald Hardrada, half-brother to St. Olaf, died in his attempt to claim England for his kingdom. The age both began and ended with violence.

That doesn't mean that there weren't adventurous Norsemen before Lindisfarne or after Stamford Bridge. The rise and fall of kingdoms is a fascinating theme of history. Some are like meteors racing across the sky. Others seem eternal. Many do not outlast their founders. Such were the kingdoms of Attila the Hun, Hitler and Mussolini. By contrast, the Roman Empire seemed destined to last forever, whether in Rome or Constantinople.

Once the Viking outbreak took place from Denmark, Norway and Sweden, it achieved a reputation of terror as it moved with the element of surprise against unsuspecting neighbors. But it wasn't long before these Norsemen had gained a foothold in England, Ireland, France, the North Sea Islands and along the rivers of Russia. After their swift rise in the ninth and tenth centuries, it seemed that they might become the permanent power of the North Sea. The eleventh century saw them rise to their highest heights and then fade away.

After living for two hundred years as conquerors and settlers in Ireland, an invasion by the grandest Viking army ever assembled was defeated at the battle of Clontarf, near Dublin, on Good Friday 1014. A combined army of Irish and Norwegian-Irish fought against the foreigners who were joined by other Irish. The Irish high-king, Brian Boru, inspired his forces to victory only to die on that same day together with his heirs. Four thousand defenders and seven thousand invaders fell in one day. One of the Vikings stopped to tie his shoes during the retreat. The defenders asked him why he was not fleeing. He answered that he wouldn't be able to make it back to his home in Iceland by nightfall anyway. They let him live. And Ireland remained Irish.

Danish and Norwegian kings and other pretenders to power continually fought to rule over Norway ("North-way"). The descendants of King Harald "Finehair," the first Norwegian king to rule over the whole land, kept reappearing even though defeated by the Danes. Olaf Tryggvason was ambushed and defeated in 1000 at sea by his brother-in-law, Svein "Forkbeard." Olaf Haraldson died at Sticklestad against Knut the Great, the Danish king of England in 1030. Their sons, Magnus Olafson and Hordaknut Knutson divided the lands and agreed that if one should die the other would inherit all. Magnus was the survivor.

Magnus' uncle, Harald Hardrada (half brother of St. Olaf), returned from his adventures in Russia and Constantinople and secured half the kingdom from Magnus. Shortly afterwards Magnus died. Harald and Svein, Knut's nephew, agreed to divide Norway and Denmark between then. Then Harald Hardrada sailed off to England to conquer the land when the English king, Harald Godwinson, the grandson of a Viking, claimed the throne in 1066. Harald Hardrada, the greatest warrior of his time, fell at the battle of Stamford Bridge when his troops were caught napping in the sun. A couple of weeks later, new conquerors arrived in the south of England from Normandy under the leadership of Duke William, a descendant of Vikings. That was the end of Viking pretensions to England.

When Jaroslav died in Russia in 1054, the Viking character of the rulers in Kiev came to an end. For over two hundred years their ships had plied the waters of the Russian rivers to deal in furs and slaves. No longer would they dream of a Viking kingdom among the Slavs.

The Normans would be dominant for a while in southern Italy, Sicily and especially England. But they had become French in their language and ways. While they have had a permanent influence on England, the island country returned to its Anglo-Saxon heritage after a few generations.

The Viking settlers in Iceland maintained their heritage. They settled down to be farmers for the most part. Some of them had gone on to Greenland and a few had explored the northeast coasts of North America. But they never had political influence in other Norse lands.

What caused the downfall of the Viking kingdoms? Prof. Gwyn Jones, from Cardiff University in Wales, has given four reasons in his book *A History of the Vikings*. First, "the constant struggle for territory and dominance in and between the three homeland kingdoms" (Denmark, Norway and Sweden); second, "their general inability to propagate elsewhere their political, social, and religious systems;" third, "the fact that they must encounter nations and people, the Franks and English, the Empire, Byzantium, the (Moslem) Caliphates, and in the long run the Slavs, richer or stronger, and altogether more absorbent and self-renewing than themselves;" and fourth, "most important of all, their lack of manpower."

Prof. Jones' analysis of the Viking's demise is on target. The Norsemen were never properly organized for long term conquest and they overextended themselves. They were typical of the Germanic tribes that gathered about a leader who for all practical purposes "owned" the country. When the leader died, they had to start all over again to build new loyalties. One reason that the Roman empire lasted so long is that it had a mystique about being a nation with a destiny. Emperors were crowned and often assassinated, but the nation lived on with its code of law.

In America, the constitution is the staying power of government. Even presidents may resign, but the nation remains intact. While the Vikings had a strong sense of democracy in their homelands based on their "Things" (assemblies), the only place that they effectively transplanted it to was Iceland, a land practically uninhabited when they arrived. They never made their style of democracy work in any other land. On the contrary, they were assimilated into the local population and changed language, religion and social customs. Nowhere did they rise to greater leadership achievements than in Normandy.

So what happened to these Vikings? They became "Christian" Danes, Norwegians and Swedes in their homelands. I've asked people in Scandinavia today about their Viking past and they prefer not to talk about it. They regard the Viking age as one of heathen barbarism which they reject today. It appears to me that it's chiefly in America that the pagan Viking past is glamorized. Of course, some of the old names of the pagan gods are still around. You'll find Scandinavian lodges with names like Odin and Thor and personal names like Thor, Thordis, Thorson or Thoreson, Thorvald, Torgerson, etc. still persist. My maternal grandfather was born Thoreson, but changed his name to Thompson in America. So did a lot of others.

Nations rise and fall, sometimes swiftly. President Lincoln referred to our constitutional freedoms in his Gettysburg Address when he said, "Now we are engaged in a great civil war, testing whether that nation, or any nation so conceived and dedicated, can long endure."

The Viking power lasted about 250 years. That's a lot longer than their Christian neighbors wished. Today they've become the world's foremost advocates of peace. Who would have guessed it?

Remnants of bygone days.

CHAPTER 53

Going To Church
In Scandinavia

SINCE EARLY CHILDHOOD, it was one my dreams to worship at the Nidaros Cathedral in Trondheim. Having expected the formal high mass, I was surprised at the simplicity of the service. It was during the summer and we sat in chairs facing an altar in the middle. We sang hymns the best we could without hymnals. We listened to scripture, prayers and a sermon. After the service, I began to look the building over, but was called back by an usher who said we'd have to return at two o'clock for the tour. On a visit some years later, we worshipped in the main sanctuary and found the hymnals. Even though nobody greeted us, asked who we were or any of those things we do in America, it was still exciting to be where St. Olaf had been buried.

The friendliest service was in English at Stockholm's St. Klara's Church. The pastor was a Swedish-American from California. At the close, we were asked to identify the countries and were invited to the parish hall for coffee and pastries. We felt ourselves to be a part of the church universal.

Another time, we stopped with a group at the Grundtvig Church in Copenhagen. It's built in modern Danish architecture and looks like a pipe organ. We came early to see it and wanted to have time for prayers. While admiring the beautiful interior, an usher appeared and told us to leave. The tour guide was warned never to do that again! You'd have thought that we were trying to steal the place. So we went back to the motor coach and held our service, remembering both Denmark and the Grundtvig Church.

Scandinavians typically have very private feelings about worship. Visitors get no jolly handshakes at the door. However, if you attend a smaller church with friends, it is quite different. At Bindslev, a small city in Jutland (northern Denmark), we worshipped in a cordial, though reserved, setting. After the service, we walked through the cemetery, looking up family gravestones and ended up at the pastor's house for breakfast. At the older

177

church in Bindslev, the religious paintings on the walls which had been covered up with whitewash since the Reformation 450 years earlier were being restored. These were considered too "Catholic" then, but now are prized for their beauty and antiquity.

The Mo Church in Surnadal (Norway) is triangular in design and is painted red. The pews have gates and each family knows where they are supposed to sit. We saw the font where my paternal ancestors had been baptized and we kneeled at the altar where my grandfather had communed before going to America in 1892. Mothers of children being baptized wore bunads (the formal dress-up for the community).

Scandinavia has Lutheran "state" churches to which over ninety percent of the people belong. Though financially supported by the government for local ministry, Scandinavians contribute generously to missions and relief projects. There is complete religious freedom. Other churches include Methodist, Baptist, Roman Catholic, Pentecostal and Jewish, besides Lutherans who are independent of the state church. If you visit Scandinavia, be sure to attend church services, whether in the native language or English. It's a part of the heritage.

CHAPTER 54

Folk Tales
Of Scandinavia

"FOLKTALES" ARE AMONG THE OLDEST of stories in the world. They are, however, often confused with fairy tales. Fairy tales, also called "wonder tales," are full of supernatural marvels and usually take place in make-believe places. Folktales are legends or sagas from the lives of real people and places. They are based on beliefs which were accepted by the social group in which they were told. They are also relevant to the concerns that people felt about the meaning of life. They belong to the realm of what really happens in this world rather than imaginary. The story teller believed that they happened and expected the listeners to accept them as true.

Some legends are "local" in character, relating to a specific geographical place. Others are "migratory." They could be told as happening in a variety of places. These stories are different in their world view from the scientifically oriented world in which we live. But it has not been so many years ago when the truths claimed by these stories were accepted as facts in the communities where they were told. And even when people no longer believed the legends, they still liked to tell them, especially to children. Folk tales are usually overladen with moral lessons.

In the Swedish countryside, there was supposed to have been a great church bell which had many coins visibly imbedded into it while being cast. It happened that while the metal for the bell was in the smelter that a certain Lady Wallron was passing by. She dropped an apron full of silver coins into the molten metal, saying whenever the bell rang it would say her name, "Wallron." The craftsman had been drunk when the lady came by so he was not tending to his job. When he saw the bell and struck it, he became so angry at the unmelted coins and their loud sound that he killed his apprentice. Still the bell sang, "Wall-ron." It was not allowed that a country bell should ring louder than a city bell, so one day someone knocked a hole in it.

There were many tales about St. Olaf whose shrine was the third most visited in medieval Europe. It was told that trolls were chasing the king to kill him because he was a Christian. The only way of escape was to spur his horse over a cliff and across the fjord. When the horse landed on a rock at the other side, the hoofs made imprints three inches deep. People believed that a nearby rock which resembled a tower was one of the trolls which Olaf changed into a stone. Because it resembled a parson wearing a cloak, people called it "The Priest." In modern times the stone was dynamited to make way for a highway.

In Denmark, we are told, a church was being built in Hadderup. Trolls came every night and smashed what the workmen built during the day. The only way to make peace with the trolls was to agree that the first woman that came to the church as a bride would belong to them. Sure enough, one day a bridal party came from another community past the Hadderup church. A thick, black fog arose. When it cleared, the bride was gone. It was claimed that bridal parties afterwards make a long detour to avoid the Hadderup church.

In a fierce battle of the Danevirke on the border of Denmark and Germany (Slesvig), it looked like the Danes were going to be defeated. The young Danish king was inexperienced in battle and ignored the advice of his commanders. Then suddenly there appeared a tall, slim lady on a snow-white horse, dressed in black. Her face was veiled as she spoke: "Shame on him who will not follow me." The Danes took courage and the enemy fled. Then she vanished. The soldiers believed that it must have been the late Queen Thyra, the wife of old king Gorm. She is believed to have influenced her son Harald to "make Denmark Christian."

In medieval Iceland the story was told about a priest who was fond of merry-making in the church, especially on Christmas eve. He delayed the Mass and continued the dancing, drinking and gambling. His old mother, Una, came three times to the church to plead with him to stop the merriment and get on with the service. As she returned to her house, a voice warned her of catastrophe, saying, "There'll be none left but Una." She saw a fearful looking man outside the church. Believing him to be the devil, she hurried to find a neighboring priest to save her son. But it was too late.

When they returned, the church had sunk into the ground and she could hear the wailing of the people from deep underground. A new church was built some distance away, but there was no dancing in it on Christmas Eve.

Petter Daas was a well known priest in Norway and was famous for being an outstanding preacher. This was during the time when Denmark ruled over the land. One day Petter received a command from the king in Copenhagen to preach for him on Christmas Day. The text would be on the pulpit. But he had only a few hours to get there. This didn't stop Petter. He called for a "spirit of the air" to carry him to Denmark. The carrier, however, demanded as his price that he could claim the souls of all who fell asleep during the sermon. It was agreed. The church was already full when Petter arrived. The sheet of paper on the pulpit was blank – no text. So Petter said: "Out of nothing God created the world!" and preached a sermon so forceful that it held everyone's attention. No one fell asleep and the devil got no souls that day.

One of my favorite stories is how St. Olaf got the cathedral built in Trondheim. It's one of the finest churches in the world. The problem was to get a spire put on it. That was beyond Olaf's skill, so he offered the sun to whomever could complete the task. When no man was able, a troll who lived nearby offered to complete the church. The troll demanded that Olav would not say his name, assuming that he could not learn it. Olaf didn't want the troll to get the sun, so he set about to learn his name. Sailing along a cliff one night, he heard an old woman singing, "Heaven's Gold (the sun) when Tvaester came home." Olaf arrived just as the spire was put in place. He shouted: "Tvaester! You've set the vane too far to the west!" Immediately upon hearing his name, the troll fell dead on the ground. The real truth is, however, that the church was not built until 1070, forty years after Olaf's death.

These are the kinds of stories that Scandinavians told in the old days. Not only Scandinavia, but all countries have their favorites. This was their entertainment and these stories also contributed to their view of the world. They fostered fear in the listeners and prolonged the superstitious beliefs that had survived since days immemorial. It affirmed their fear that God's chief delight is to punish sinners.

181

There is something naturally appealing in these stories as there is a degree of residual guilt in almost everyone. The humor in the stories can be harsh and dark. But it reflected the mood of the people in that isolated part of the world. People today may not take ghosts and magic seriously like those people did, but they are often in bondage to modern superstitions of their own making.

CHAPTER 55

Scandinavian
Humor

TELLING STORIES OF ETHNIC HUMOR is an international sport, but it can also be a risky business. More than one person in high places has lost a good paying job because of telling a joke about an ethnic group that doesn't relish that kind of treatment.

It is generally agreed, however, that having a sense of humor is a sign of good health. It may be painful at times, but it can also be a cathartic, a cleansing experience from having your guard up all the time. The benefit of laughter is to provide relief from tension.

Immigrants have often been the target of humor. Because they spoke a different language and made obvious mistakes when speaking English, wore strange looking clothes, and could be hoodwinked easily by any shyster or prankster, people laughed at them and called them stupid. They were also described as dirty, lazy, sexually naive and foul smelling. To escape such ridicule, many of them jumped into the "melting pot" upon arrival in the New World and refused to teach their children anything about the Old World, including the language they had left behind.

I've lived in a lot of places where certain ethnic groups were the butt of jokes. Like folk tales, ethnic jokes have a way of travelling about. The same stories are told in different communities about different groups. Humor, and ethnic humor in particular, can be an aggressive, if not hostile, form of communication. It is frequently cruel. Actually, humor is accomplished by a trick of logic called "juxtaposition" in moving from the sublime to the ridiculous. A classic example is about the doctor who comforts a patient by saying, "You have a very serious disease. Of ten persons who catch it, only one survives. It's lucky you came to me, for I have recently had nine patients with this disease and they all died of it." The response evokes laughter, but also covers up pain.

My father-in-law, born in Denmark, used to tell some of the Danish jokes. These were about "other" Danes who lived in neighboring communities. Needless to say, they fit all the characteristics of an ethnic joke which made the other person a "fall guy." The Swedes in America also tell ethnic jokes, often about Norwegians.

The use of ethnic jokes, when told by the ethnic group about itself, can be an effective way to communicate truth. A favorite ploy of some people today is to tell Hittite stories, an ethnic group that lost its identity 2,500 years ago. It so happens that the names of these Hittites are Ole and Sven.

The Scandinavians have another kind of ethnic story, called "skroner." These are fables (fibs) that "could be true." John Sorensen, a Methodist pastor friend who lives in Florida, shared with me his favorite skroner. It goes like this. "Happy St. Olaf's day (July 29) and hold the anchovies! What's so special about St. Olaf? As the inventor of pizza, St. Olaf should be just about the most popular guy around. St. Olaf and pizza? Well, St. Olaf an ingenious Viking seafarer, made his claim to fame during a trip to Italy.

"One Thursday morning, a group of local farmers, greatly troubled by a tomato worm infestation, came to Olaf's beach cabin seeking help. Olaf rose to the occasion and carefully mapped a plan for driving the tomato worms from Italy by placing pieces of lutefisk at the base of every tomato plant. It worked. Unfortunately, without the worms eating holes in the plants, a bumper crop of tomatoes became a glut on the market. Tempers flared.

"It was a long-shot brainstorm that led the quick-witted Viking to invent a fast-food item that would use up the surplus crop – pizza. Lefse, tomato sauce and leftovers from the day before were combined to form a taste treat Italy fell in love with and took as her own." End of "skrone."

A few people have capitalized on ethnic jokes. Red Stangeland of Sioux Falls claims to have sold over 700,000 copies of his books. Another chronicler is Charlene Power of Crosby, North Dakota, with her series of "Uff-da" books. A native of Brookings, South Dakota, and of English and Irish origins, Charlene's claim to write these stories is that her husband (Charles) is half Scandinavian.

Charlene got her start on a radio station in 1968. She played music, reported news of the area and interviews. She also sold advertising and was the general manager. Listeners to the radio would send her their favorite jokes. I think they just liked to have their ethnic group mentioned, regardless of what was said. This was part of the popularity of Garrison Keillor's radio broadcast.

As far as I know, we humans are the only creatures that concern ourselves with ethnic humor. And for some it "pays."

CHAPTER 56

The Scandinavian
Dedication To Freedom

THIS STORY WAS TOLD ABOUT THE VIKINGS as they were advancing up-river towards Paris. The Franks sent a messenger to ask, "Who is your leader?" The Vikings replied: "We have no leader. We are all equals."

There may be a lot of folklore to this story, but there's some truth in it too. Since pre-Christian times, the people especially of Scandinavia have kept the ideal of freedom alive. It's true that they owned foreign slaves, but they were not slaves to each other. During the days of medieval feudalism in Europe, Norway and Sweden escaped the oppressive social structures which denied individual rights.

Being so far north, Scandinavians have had a feeling for independence and freedom that was unknown in the balmy lands of the Mediterranean. This dedication to freedom seems in-bred among them. To this day, if they have any great fault, it would be that they go to great lengths to protect the rights of the criminals. The exception to this was the retribution they dealt to Nazi collaborators in Denmark and Norway after World War II.

The Battle of Stickelstad on July 29, 1030, was fought between Olaf Haraldson and soldiers in the service of the Danish king of England, Knut the Great. Olaf was greatly outnumbered and was killed, but emerged as "St. Olaf." In his own way, Olaf thought of himself as a serious minded Christian who was on a missionary crusade. Many opposed him, however, for his style of leadership more than for his religion. While the coming of Christianity to Scandinavia ultimately advanced the cause of individual freedom, it did not happen immediately.

Many early Christian kings, patterning their rule after the Holy Roman Emperors, especially Charlemagne, imagined themselves to be Christian Caesars. It reached its most autocratic stage under Denmark's King Frederick III (1648-1670), when he established an "absolute monarchy" in 1661. Denmark finally received

187

constitutional law on June 5, 1849, from King Frederick. Sweden received a new constitution in 1809. Norway adopted its constitution in 1814, through a daring act of trying to achieve independence. This, however, did not happen until 1905, when it peaceably separated from the Swedish Crown.

The ancient Scandinavian form of government was the "Thing" or "Ting," an assembly of free men who made the decisions for the community. They had the power to banish those who broke the law. That's how Leif Erikson and his father were exiled to new lands in the West. Even kings were subject to having their authority ratified by the Things. There was a constant power struggle between kings and Thing leaders. As kings gained the upper hand, the local assemblies lost power. The word "Thing" is found in the name of the parliaments in Sweden's Riksdag, Denmark's "Folketing," Iceland's "Althing," Norway's "Storting," and the "Tynwald" on the Isle of Man off the south coast of England. The Scandinavian commitment to democracy today is an ancient inheritance that has been restored in modern times with encouragement from the American constitution of 1787.

Peter Brent in his book *The Viking Saga*, claims that Western civilization's ideal of democracy is more indebted to Scandinavia than to Athens and the influence of Pericles. He claimed that the Vikings, despite their unfavorable reports by church historians, were the influence that led to the democratic form of government that came to prevail in both England and America. He claims that the democratic ideal went underground in England during the oppressive rule of the Normans (Scandinavian-Frenchmen) and their feudalism.

Brent calls the English Revolution of the 1640s a popular movement that stemmed from the ancient Vikings and Anglo-Saxons (from southern Denmark and northwest Germany). The Anglo-Saxon "Moot" was similar to the Scandinavian "Thing." Brent states, "Some of the most solidly-established democracies of the modern world can thus trace their direct development back to such Scandinavian and Germanic roots, however much that development has been modified by the ideas and the vocabulary of ancient Greece." He traces the Common Law and jury system of the England to the "Things" and "Moots."

Brent notes that the trade guilds of Norsemen were voluntary associations and states "the very existence of the guilds seems to prove the depth and maturity of Scandinavian liberty, maintained through the centuries when royal power grew, an alternative to the hierarchies of feudalism, founding a tradition kept sinewy and supple even until today." Brent concludes: "It is to the Saxons and above all the Vikings, it seems to me, that the peoples of northwest Europe are truly indebted, and it is their stubborn conviction that the personal liberty of each free man is sacred which underlies our own."

The claim, "we are all equals," has a price to pay. The danger is anarchy. The strong nations of the world have always been led by dynamic leaders, for better or for worse. World wide conquest does not seem to have been the Viking goal. Those Norsemen were more interested in pirating, trading, and colonizing than having a tightly structured world empire. Being "equals," the Vikings would not tolerate a hereditary "Caesar" in their midst. They were crude and their reported cruelty is indefensible by our modern sense of justice. However, by the standards of their own generations, they probably were no more cruel than the barbarities common to the times. Our modern weaponry cannot claim gentility either.

Whatever else you may wish to think or say about those people from the North, they did prize freedom and managed to preserve it through all sorts of situations. If you should visit their lands today, take note how they still treasure freedom as the highest of human values and watch for the Nobel Peace Prize issued each October. The Vikings have finally come of age in promoting freedom for all people.

CHAPTER 57

Scandinavian Immigrant Worship Traditions

I MMIGRANTS LEAVING SCANDINAVIA for the New World received little sympathy and support from the established churches of their lands. They did not, however, abandon their faith and religious upbringing. Most of them remembered their instruction in Bible and catechism. They held a veneration for the church building, respect for an educated and ordained clergy and a sense of order and beauty in worship.

Since ninety-eight percent of the people from Scandinavian countries during the immigration period regarded themselves as members of the Evangelical Lutheran Church, large numbers became attached to new Lutheran congregations on the American frontier. There were, however, some who had joined non-Lutheran congregations while still in Europe, namely Methodists, Baptists and Swedish Covenant. The Scandinavians were unprepared for the religious diversity of the American frontier. Many joined whatever denomination happened to be handy and often lost contact with their Scandinavian heritage.

Large numbers of Swedish immigrants became a part of the Augustana Synod. Significant numbers also joined congregations of the Evangelical Covenant Church.

Danes often joined another ethnic Lutheran group or become a part of the American "melting pot." The Norwegians were the most likely of the Scandinavians to join a Lutheran congregation. One reason is that they were divided into several Lutheran denominations and often isolated from other people.

The Finns and Icelandic people also established their own denominations. Ever since 1890, merger movements have been prominent among Scandinavian Lutherans and in 1988 it became virtually complete in the newly formed "Evangelical Lutheran Church in America."

There were two basic centers of influence for worship among Scandinavian immigrants. Danish language and customs helped shape worship in Norway and Iceland. Swedish influence has been strong in Finland.

The Swedes had the most elaborate liturgy. They liked a chanted service. This was reassuring to the immigrants when they heard their services in the New World intoned with the familiar sounds of home. Then they felt that God was with them. The Finns also preferred the chanted liturgy.

Worship among Danes has been enriched by three great hymn writers: Hans Brorson, Thomas Kingo and N. F. S. Grundtvig. More than five hundred of their hymns are still found in the current Danish hymnal, even though only fifteen are used in the *Lutheran Book of Worship* used in America. Religion among the Danes has always, even from pre-Christian times, combined personal piety and community life. This especially came to the fore in the work of Bishop Grundtvig (1783-1872). Danes like to keep their liturgies simple, with scripture, sermon and sacrament central.

Some Scandinavians employed a "klokker." This was a layman (deacon) who opened and closed the service with a prescribed prayer. No layman would presume to usurp the role of the pastor, but there was a definite place for him in worship. In America, Norwegians were the most divided between those who favored the "high mass" of Norway or a simpler order of worship. In almost all cases, the pastor was president of the congregation. In 1952 when I became pastor in North Dakota, I was also president of the congregations according to their constitutions. I arranged for the election of a lay vice president who presided at annual meetings until the constitutions could be changed.

The most familiar symbol of the Scandinavian clergy was the ruffled collar worn by the clergy in pioneer days. It's still used in Scandinavia today. On one of my visits to Scandinavia, I tried to buy one and found out that it had to be ordered from Denmark. Fortunately, a cousin in the ministry had an extra one and gave it to me. The black gown was a sign of pastoral authority from God. Bishop Bo Giertz of Gothenburg, Sweden, wrote of the importance of this garment for the pastor's exercise of the ministerial office in his book, *The Hammer of God*. Purple was often the only liturgical color used on the altar and pulpit. The Church Year was faithfully followed.

Holy communion was the most serious experience of worship. Four times a year (or less) was considered "safe." Scandinavians took repentance seriously as preparation for the sacrament. They were conditioned to be introspective about sin. However frightening, holy communion had a profound effect for spiritual healing among them. In Rølvaag's *Giants in the Earth*, Beret found sanity through the sacrament. Many Swedish Lutherans practiced fasting before communion.

Scandinavian Lutherans have emphasized congregational freedom and authority, in contrast to their German Lutheran cousins who have put more power into the hands of the bishops, pastors and councils. The concern for local authority goes back to the "Thing" assemblies of free farmers in Viking days. It's a strange fact that Scandinavia had the freest society in the ancient world. Even kings needed their approval to rule.

The immigrant church among Scandinavians was a man's domain. The role of women was to rear children, operate the Ladies Aid, teach Sunday school and keep the home. This might include milking the cows and slopping the hogs. But voting, preaching and governing was the exclusive right of men. They also sat on different sides of the aisle. These cultural characteristics of the faith have largely changed in our time, but the passion for freedom and the need to be serious still dominates Scandinavian worship life in America.

Typical Scandinavian Immigrant Church.

193

CHAPTER 58

Favorite Hymns
Of Scandinavia

MY SON, MICHAEL, while a student at Wartburg Seminary in Dubuque, Iowa, asked me, "Why don't you write a story about Scandinavian hymns?" It sounded like a good idea since the Scandinavian hymns have a distinct character and have been a powerful influence on the lives of those northern people.

I first heard these hymns sung by my father, Oscar (1903-1969), who had a beautiful tenor voice. I came to appreciate good music while listening to these hymns and nursery rhymes while I sat on his lap as a small child. The hymns were sung mostly in Norwegian. The tunes and lyrics still ring in my soul. One of the reasons that they've become so much a part of me is that they were sung to the melodic folk tunes.

Scandinavia was geographically isolated from much of the world until modern times. Now, of course, there are hardly any places that aren't heavily influenced by what is going on in the rest of the world. It was in this setting of isolation that some of the world's most beautiful folk music originated. Fortunately, many of these hymns were collected into hymnals so that we still have access to them, even if most of them aren't sung any more.

The Reformation is credited with introducing the congregational singing of hymns first in Germany. This spread to Sweden through the Petri brothers, Olavus and Laurentius. Sons of a blacksmith, they studied at Wittenberg University and brought back many of Luther's hymns to Sweden. Their fiery zeal for the new learning in Germany was not without risk, however. They might have been massacred in the Stockholm "bloodbath" of 1520, if some Germans in the city had not saved them. When the Swedish revolution of 1523 placed Gustavus Vasa on the throne, the Petri brothers were given important positions in both church and state. Most of their hymns, however, are translations of German and Latin originals.

195

Hymnody was given a great boost by the pietist movements in the Scandinavian countries. This was an appeal to a religion of the heart that emphasized "living" the faith. E. E. Ryden, in his book *The Story of our Hymns* (1930), called Johan Olof Wallin (1779-1839) "Scandinavia's greatest hymnist and perhaps the foremost in the entire Christian Church during the nineteenth century." Born into poverty and with poor health, Wallin earned a Ph. D. at Uppsala University when he was twenty-four. His poetic talent produced 128 original hymns, plus twenty-three translations and 178 revisions in the Swedish *Psalm Book* of 1819. He has been called "David's harp in the Northland."

A well known hymn of Swedish background is "Children of the Heavenly Father" (Tryggare Kan Ingen Vare) written by Lina Sandell Berg (1832-1903). She wrote 650 hymns. Her father, a parish pastor, drowned when the ship on which they were travelling gave a sudden lurch and he fell overboard. She discovered her comfort in writing hymns. Her hymns were popularized by Jenny Lind, known as the "Swedish Nightingale."

Another Swedish hymn which has become popular in America is "How Great Thou Art" (Den Store Gud), written by Carl Boberg (1850-1940). Inspiration for the hymn came one evening when he was struck by the beauty of nature and the sound of church bells. The Swedes have popularized a Christmas hymn of German origin so that almost everyone thinks it's a Swedish carol, "When Christmas Morn is Dawning" (Nar Juldagsmorgon Glimmar).

Denmark's three most famous hymn writers were all bishops. Hans Brorson (1694-1764) wrote a Christmas hymn that I remember from earliest childhood "Your Little Ones, Dear Lord, Are We" (Her Komme Dine Arme Smaa). I can still choke up while singing it in Danish each Christmas. Brorson wrote the best loved of all the hymns of Norway, "Den Store Hvide Flok." We use it so frequently in the original that it's hardly sung in the translation, "Behold, a Host." The music, based on a Norse folk tune from Heddal (home of Norway's largest stave church), was arranged by Edvard Grieg (1843-1907), Norway's most famous musician.

While visiting the St. Magnus' Cathedral in Odense on the island of Fyen, I saw the statue of Thomas Hansen Kingo 1634-1703), the first great hymn writer of Denmark. Two of his hymns, "On My Heart Imprint Your Image" and "All Who Believe and are Baptized" are sung in many American churches today. His paternal family had come from Scotland, as had Edvard Grieg's.

The greatest hymnwriter of Denmark was Nikolai Severin Fredrik Grundtvig (1783-1872). Two of his Christmas hymns are sung every year, "The Bells of Christmas" (Det Kimer nu til Julefest) and "O How Beautiful the Sky" (Dejlig er den Himmel Blaa). Of the one thousand hymns he wrote, two of them frequently sung today are "Built on a Rock" (Kirken den er et Gammelt Hus) and "O Day Full of Grace" (Den Signede Dag). Grundtvig was also famous for his work of establishing "folk schools" which were forerunners to public education in Denmark.

Iceland's most famous hymnwriter was Valdimar Briem (1848-1930). He is remembered in America by his hymn "How Marvellous God's Greatness." One of Iceland's hymns which became its national anthem, "O Gud Vors Lands" (O God of our Land), was written by Matthias Jochumsson (1835-1920).

Finland's most celebrated musician, Jean Sibelius, is best known for his "Finlandia." It's the tune used for the hymn, "Thee God, We Praise." Among the Finnish hymns used in America are J. L. Runeberg's (1804-1877) "I Lift My Eyes Unto Heaven;" "Your Kingdom Come, O Father" by Kauko-Veikko Tamminen (1882-1946); and "Lost in the Night" from an unknown secular source. The Finns have contributed many more tunes to which hymns have been set.

Norway's mountains, valleys and fjords have been an inspiration to many musicians, including hymn writers. The best known Christmas carol from Norway is "Jeg er saa glad" (I Am So Glad Each Christmas Eve) written by Marie Wexelsen (1832-1911). Two of the greatest names in Norwegian church music are M. B. Landstad (1802-1880) and Ludvig M. Lindemann (1812-1887). Landstad's hymnals were found in nearly every trunk that came with Norwegians to America. The hymn for which he is best known in America is "I Know of a Sleep in Jesus' Name."

Lindemann's original family name was Madsen, which may have been Danish. His grandfather, a physician in Trondheim, changed his name to Lindemann (German). This was a popular thing to do about two hundred years ago. (I have discovered people of my ancestry in Norway who changed their name to Fische.) Lindemann wrote the music for many hymns including "Come to Calvary's Holy Mountain," "Built on a Rock," "Jesus Priceless Treasure" and "Hallelujah! Jesus Lives!"

Besides "Den Store Hvide Flok," hymns that I remember my father singing to me as a small child include "I Himmelen, I Himmelen" (In Heaven Above) and "Velt Alle Dine Veie." The words of the latter still speak to me, "Thy way and all thy sorrows, give thou into his hand. His gracious care unfailing, who doth the heavens command. Their course and path he giveth to clouds and air and wind. A way thy feet may follow; he, too, for thee will find." It's been over two decades since my father last sang among us. His love for Scandinavian hymnody has been an enriching legacy.

There was an enduring quality to these hymns and we'd do well to take a second look at them today. And if given a chance, many of the tunes would keep singing in our minds and hearts forever.

CHAPTER 59

The Scandinavian
Colleges In America

"HOW THEY LOVE EDUCATION. How they will plan and how ready they are to sacrifice and to suffer that their children may have an education. I actually saw large families living in sod shacks on the open prairie sending a boy or a girl to Concordia College." This is how Rev. George H. Gerberding, newly arrived from the East in Fargo, North Dakota, described the Scandinavian passion for education.

The Scandinavian immigration to America happened when an awakening to learning was taking place in their homelands. Sweden's new ruling family, the Bernadottes from France, embraced the creed of liberty, equality and fraternity. Norway had recently gotten a university. Bishop Grundtvig was leading a movement in Denmark to make education available for the common people. Finland was just reclaiming its own language for literature and government after hundreds of years of Swedish dominance.

It was only natural that education was such a high priority in the minds of so many Scandinavian immigrants. The earliest Scandinavian school, named Augustana, began at Chicago in 1860. Being a joint venture of Swedish and Norwegian congregations, its primary concern was to prepare the sons of immigrants for the ministry. Times were tough. In 1862, the school was lured to Paxton, Illinois, by an offer of the Illinois Central Railroad. In 1869, the Norwegians set up their own school and parted from the Swedes as friends.

From these humble beginnings came Augustana (Swedish) College in Rock Island, Illinois, and Augustana (Norwegian) College in Sioux Falls, South Dakota, and Augsburg College (also Norwegian) in Minneapolis. "Augsburg," the German name for Augustana (Latin), refers to the "Augsburg Confession," a statement of faith accepted by Lutherans. Other Swedish schools include Gustavus Adolphus (1862), St. Peter, Minnesota; Bethany

(1881), Lindsborg, Kansas; Uppsala (1893), East Orange, New Jersey, and Bethel (Baptist) in St. Paul.

The Norwegians founded Luther College in 1861, when the Union Army closed down Concordia Seminary in St. Louis, because the faculty were said to be sympathetic to slavery. Prior to this, the Norwegian Synod leaders had visited several Lutheran schools and were impressed by the educational system of the Missouri Synod Lutherans. They arranged for some Norwegian faculty to be at Concordia Seminary to tutor the future Norwegian pastors. While the Norwegian faculty in St. Louis favored the arrangement and even defended its views on slavery, the Norwegian congregations would have no part of it. They began a school near LaCrosse, Wisconsin, in a vacant parsonage which moved the following year to Decorah, Iowa. This is the present Luther College.

Later Norwegian schools started in Minnesota were St. Olaf (1874) at Northfield and Concordia (1891) at Moorhead. Pacific Lutheran University (1891) was founded in Tacoma, Washington. Waldorf College (1903) in Forest City, Iowa, Camrose Lutheran College (1911) in Camrose, Alberta, and Luther College (1913) in Regina, Saskatchewan followed after the turn of the century. There had also been a Clifton College in Clifton, Texas, which was merged with Texas Lutheran at Seguin in 1954. Bethany College, Mankato, Minnesota, was started by Norwegian-Americans in 1926. Scandinavian-Americans were also active in starting California Lutheran College at Thousand Oaks near Los Angeles in 1961.

The Danes started two colleges which are still in operation: Dana (1884) in Blair, Nebraska and Grand View (1896) in Des Moines, Iowa. Suomi College in Hancock, Michigan, was begun in 1896 by Finnish immigrants. Besides the above named schools, there were many more smaller colleges and academies (high schools) operated by Scandinavians which have either been merged into larger schools or were closed by the great depression of the 1930s. The only one of those academies operating today in the United States is Oak Grove Lutheran High School in Fargo, North Dakota, where I received my high school diploma.

What was the driving force behind this passion for education? The Scandinavians were aliens in a strange and not always hospitable land. Establishing schools helped them to retain their ethnic identity and to keep their religious faith as taught in their homelands. It made it possible for many farm youth to get an education with limited ability in English. Since many communities did not have high schools, the academies with a college department provided dormitories and made an education possible for many immigrant children.

Most of the schools started by Scandinavians have chosen not to become universities. There was a movement in the 1950s to make this change. The decision to remain "colleges" prevailed because it was thought better to be colleges of excellence. The decision has been vindicated. The Scandinavian-American colleges now serve people of all ethnic backgrounds, but they have not forgotten their heritage.

CHAPTER 60

'Odin's Ravens' And
The Scandinavian Press

T HE OLD NORSE GOD, ODIN, was way ahead of his time. He had a great passion for information and knowledge, even sacrificing one of his eyes for more knowledge. In order to keep informed about the events of the world, he had two ravens which sat on each of his shoulders. Their names were Hugin and Munin. Each morning he sent them out to fly all over the world and they'd return to his home in Valhalla each evening. Then they'd report to him all that they had seen and heard.

Odin would have been interested in our "information age" and would have taken a keen interest in the way the press operates today in Scandinavia. The three hundred-year history of the Nordic press has had a lot to do with promoting democracy in those lands.

Printing presses reached Sweden in 1483 and Iceland in 1526. In 1624 a news sheet entitled *Hermes Gothicus* was published for King Gustavus Adolphus. Denmark had Scandinavia's first public newspaper in 1634.

Freedom of the press is a high concern for any democracy. The First Amendment to the United States Constitution (1787) states that "Congress shall make no law . . . abridging the freedom of speech, or of the press." Sweden had such a law in 1766. The principle of citizen rights has been a part of the Scandinavian heritage since before Christian times when they had local assemblies (Things) at which every free man had the right of speech and a vote.

Sweden has strict laws protecting the public from scandal. They've created an "Ombudsman" position which acts as a citizen advocate to protect people's rights against government bureaucracy. If a person is accused of breaking a law in Sweden, it's illegal to mention the name in the media. The name is protected from publication until conviction. This is to protect a person's reputation and to assist in rehabilitation. Libel suits against editors are not as numerous in Scandinavia as in America, partly because the awards are small and the plaintiff's risk is high. It includes paying the editor's legal costs.

The Swedish king tried to suppress *Aftonbladet* (published in Stockholm) for its liberal views. Each time it was banned, it reappeared with a new name such as *Aftonbladet the Second*, *Aftonbladet the Third*, etc. After 14 such attempts, the harassment stopped. *Aftonbladet* was regarded as the "Bible of the Swedish people."

Expressen, a Liberal Party paper published in Stockholm with a circulation of 531,000, is the largest Scandinavian newspaper. It's followed closely by *Helsingin Sanomat*, a conservative paper with a circulation of 450,000 published in Helsinki. The largest newspaper in Norway today is *Aftenposten* with a circulation of 230,000. It publishes both morning and afternoon editions with a conservative point of view. While having only the eighth largest circulation in Scandinavia, *Aftenposten* is regarded as the most influential, followed by the conservative *Berlingske Tidende* (Denmark's oldest, founded in 1749), and Sweden's *Dagens Nyheter*, an independent paper with a centrist political position.

Finland was dependent on Swedish as its cultural language until the mid-nineteenth century. It wasn't until 1847 that a Finnish language newspaper appeared in Helsinki. This was during the Russian period (1809-1917). Three years later, the Czars started to impose a strict censorship. They managed to get some freedom of the press by 1855. However, about 1900, in the latter days of the Czarist rule, the government again imposed heavy censorship.

The Norwegian constitution of 1814 provided for freedom of the press. The constitution reads: "There shall be liberty of the press. No person shall be punished for any writing . . . unless he willfully and manifestly has either himself shown or incited others to disobedience to the laws, or resistance to their orders, or has advanced false and defamatory accusations against another person." Only rarely will a journalist have to identify a source in Scandinavia.

Morgenbladet, a morning newspaper founded in 1819, is the oldest Norwegian newspaper. Because of its liberal political views, circulation was forbidden in Denmark. The word "liberal" in Norway meant that they wanted their political independence. Denmark didn't have a constitution until 1849 when freedom of the press became guaranteed.

Dagbladet is a daily Norwegian tabloid with a circulation of 140,000. They like the articles about entertainment and highly sensational stories with lots of pictures.

Iceland got its first daily newspaper in 1910. The Icelandic people are the most interested in world news of all the Scandinavians. Their little island republic depends on international connections.

During World War I, both the British and German governments tried to influence political views in the Swedish press. The Swedes resisted these attempts in their determination to be neutral. The role of the newspaper in Sweden has been described as being a "watchdog" on the government.

Scandinavian newspapers are privately owned as in America, but many of the weeklies have government subsidies so they can inform and educate the public. Norwegian newspapers have public education as their primary goal and carry a lot of essays and in-depth discussions. It's not uncommon to find carefully researched articles on philosophy, theology, history, architecture, economics, social policy and heritage in the Nordic newspapers. The newspapers often are the vehicles of public debates. They are expected to practice restraint on publishing articles that would harm the government's foreign policy, especially in Finland.

Denmark has the tradition of having a four-newspaper system: Conservative, Social Democrat, Liberal and Radical Liberal. Copenhagen has twelve daily newspapers today, whereas Chicago has only two and Minneapolis one. Scandinavians have the highest per capita readership and many homes take two or more daily newspapers. Ninety-eight of the people in Finland read a daily newspaper.

It's interesting to read the well-known American comics in the Scandinavian newspapers. Among these are Peanuts, Donald Duck, Hagar the Horrible, Sad Sack, Garfield and Blondie.

Humor, however, in a foreign language is more difficult to understand than informational reading. So a foreigner is apt to miss the punch line even when translated.

World War II was a time of special importance to newspapers in Denmark and Norway. "Underground journalism" sprang up in newspapers which were permitted to stay in business. Articles were written in such a clever way that the Nazis had difficulty catching on to what was being said between the lines. There were over 300 underground papers circulating in Norway during the War.

Patriotic newspapers were operating all over Denmark during the occupation. One hundred and sixty-six newspapers with a circulation of 2,600,000 were printed in 1943. In 1944 the Nazis made mass arrests of journalists and printers. The Communist newspaper was banned, but it also went underground. Oppression increased the newspapers to 244 with an incredible circulation of 11,000,000. Since the war, the number of newspapers has declined but the readership has remained high.

My favorite story of the war in Denmark was when the British bombed the rail yards at Fredrikshavn in northern Jutland. The Nazis ordered the newspapers to report that the bombs fell harmlessly in a pasture killing a cow. Two days later, the press reported that "the cow that was killed in the R. A. F. raid two days ago is still burning." The Danes used ridicule as an effective weapon against the invaders.

If Odin were around today, he'd be reading newspapers too, besides tuning in on all news radio and television stations. But then, what would he do with his ravens?

An excellent study on Scandinavian newspapers is *The Ravens of Odin: The Press in the Nordic Nations* by Robert G. Picard (State University of Iowa Press, 1988).

CHAPTER 61

Flying With The
Scandinavian Airline System

T HERE ARE MANY GOOD AIRLINES and several which
travel to Scandinavia. None of them, however, is structured like the "Scandinavian Air System." SAS is a con-
sortium owned by the Danish, Norwegian and Swedish
Airlines. The parent companies are owned fifty/fifty by government and private shareholders.

We weren't long on the plane before we could feel the
Scandinavian atmosphere. Flight announcements were made on a
movie screen with pictures of Copenhagen. The predominance of
blonde cabin attendants and gentle accents left no doubt that we
had already entered Scandinavia, even though we were still on
the runway.

Taking off at 5:30 p.m. from Chicago's O'Hare International
Airport, we landed eight hours later (8:30 a.m.) in Copenhagen.
Our DC-10 flight #942 covered 3,850 miles at 550 MPH at an alti-
tude of 33,000 feet. We had a clear view of Norway's west coast
near Stavanger as we began our approach to Denmark. After talking with the Purser (chief steward), I was given the Flight Map
with flight data posted for the passengers.

In charge of the flight to Denmark was Captain Sverre
Prestbakken. Visiting with him in the cockpit, I learned that he
had attended the 1985 Hallinglaget in Tacoma, Washington. I
hadn't been there, but I pulled out my membership card in the
Hallinglag to prove my ethnicity. Knowing that a Halling was in
control, I relaxed even more.

We hadn't been long in the air when a full course dinner was
served. It left nothing to be desired except a bigger appetite. The
food was prepared under the direction of Johanna and Crister
Svantesson of Gotenburg, Sweden, the home city of my good
friends Elon and Norah Eliasson, famous for their culinary skills
in New York City. Before landing, every passenger was given a

steaming-hot hand towel to freshen up for the Continental Breakfast.

On the overseas flight, headphones were distributed so that we could either listen to a choice of music or hear the sound for a movie being shown. A cart with duty-free items for sale also passed through the aisles.

SAS was founded August 1, 1946, with headquarters in Stockholm. In addition to owning an airline, it has a score of subsidiary and associated companies. One of the reasons for SAS's rapid progress is its president, Jan Carlzon. He's a gifted communicator and an innovative leader with a Master of Business Administration degree from the Stockholm School of Economics. Each year SAS serves over 10,000,000 passengers and carries about 160,000 tons of cargo to ninety cities in forty countries. Almost thirty thousand people are employed.

The SAS lounges are delightfully comfortable at the International terminals. There we could rest, enjoy refreshments, use a desk for writing or make phone calls. Our return to Chicago gave me the clearest view I've ever had of Iceland. Every roof top was visible in Reykjavik from 31,000 feet. This flight was captained by Leif Hansen from Copenhagen. It was as smooth as glass. He invited me to the cockpit to talk about SAS and to show me the instrument panels. I was impressed. To become the captain of an SAS overseas flight takes a long career in aviation.

The modern Vikings have improved a great deal on the long-ships by which they traversed the sea one thousand years ago. While the old ways must have been exciting, I prefer the new ways. We flew SAS again in 1991 to Copenhagen and on to Athens. We again experienced the same wonderful comfort and hospitality.

The Scandinavian Air System in flight.

CHAPTER 62

Golf – An 'Exploding' Sport In Scandinavia

WHEN WE LED A TOUR TO SCANDINAVIA in 1984, Paul Kemper took his golf clubs along, but he never found use for them. It just wasn't that much of a sport over there and golf courses were few and far between.

While staying in a hotel in Racine in October 1989, we discovered that a Scandinavian tour group was also staying there. That naturally got my curiosity. What brought them to this city made famous by its Danish culture?

Two large buses drove up and unloaded its passengers. I made a remark about the weather to one of them. He answered with a Danish accent. I changed over to speaking Danish and learned that he was one of ninety-two people from Scandinavia getting acquainted with how golf courses are managed in America. We were in for a surprise which led to an enjoyable visit.

They were on a two-week tour which took them first to Racine where they were the guests of the Jacobsen Corporation. The Jacobsen Corporation was started by an immigrant from Denmark. It manufactures lawn mowers and equipment for maintaining golf courses. Jacobsen has a lot of trade with Scandinavia. From there they went to Minneapolis where they visited with Don White, Chairman of the Department of Horticulture at the University of Minnesota. They also visited a sod farm near Stillwater and National Turfco, a company which deals in products used in the maintenance of golf courses. Leaving the Midwest, they travelled to Charlotte, North Carolina; and on to Orlando, Florida, to visit Disney World and the EPCOT Center; and then on to Miami and New York, inspecting golf courses at each stop.

We visited with Svend Andreasen of Esbjerg, Denmark; Erik Sorenson of Hjorring, Denmark; and Gunnor Sundstol of Kristiansand, Norway. Gunnor was the only Norwegian in the group, though there were two Swedes along who were working on golf courses in Norway. Twenty-eight of the group were from Denmark, nineteen from Finland and forty were from Sweden. All of the visitors were men except four women, two of whom were spouses of the golfing promoters. Their reason for coming to America was to get acquainted with American techniques in maintaining golf courses. The Scandinavian countries import all their golfing supplies.

We were wondering how popular golf is in Scandinavia. Gunnor told us that Norway's first golf course was built in 1925. During World War II, the Nazis ordered the golf course to be plowed up to grow vegetables. (I'm surprised that the Norwegians did not press this as one of the accusations at the War Crimes Trials in Nuremburg at the end of the war.) Today there are about twelve golf courses in Norway, with many more being planned. They hope to have fifty by the year 2000.

Denmark was the first to have a golf course in Scandinavia, having built one in 1921. There are sixty-five golf courses today but plans have been made to build ten more. They told us that many Germans come to play golf in Denmark because it's cheaper than in their own country. Golf is a rich person's game in Germany, they said, but not in Scandinavia. They were convinced that golf should be available to everyone.

Sweden has the most golf courses in Scandinavia, about two hundredwith another one hundred being planned. The Scandinavian visitors enthusiastically exclaimed that golf will be a major sport in their countries before 2000. Soccer is the major sport in Scandinavia today.

Because of its long winters, golfing in Norway is a summertime sport, but Denmark and Sweden, being further south, also have winter golf. They use the same fairways in the winter, but different greens. They told us that snow doesn't last long in southern Sweden and Denmark.

All golf courses in Scandinavia, according to those visitors, are operated as clubs. People who belong to golf clubs in any other part of the world can play in Scandinavia just for a daily green fee, about twenty dollars for all day and not just eighteen holes.

They were surprised that we had open golfing for non-members golf in America. They asked, "How will people learn the rules if they are not taught?" We explained that people in America may take golf for credit in high school and college, or just learn from a friend. This seemed a bit strange to them.

A membership in a Danish golf club costs about $300 a year, plus the initiation fee. They were quite shocked to learn how expensive belonging to a country club can be in America. Hjorring has one course of nine holes, but was being enlarged to eighteen. They expected to have 650 members by 1990. Esbjerg had 1,100 members with three hundred on the waiting list. This usually takes about two years to gain membership. Many people from Great Britain also come to play golf in Denmark.

Just how popular is golf becoming in Scandinavia? They told us it was "exploding." So if you are a golfer, pack your clubs the next time you travel to Scandinavia.